D1201322

Relative frequency
of
English spellings

Relative frequency of English spellings

by

Godfrey Dewey, Ed.D.

TEACHERS COLLEGE PRESS

Teachers College, Columbia University
New York

Library of Congress Catalog Card Number: 71-118887

Manufactured in the United States of America

Foreword

For fifty years, Dr. Godfrey Dewey has continued to make significant contributions to our understandings of orthography. He early investigated two crucial facets of orthography: 1) conventional spellings used to represent speech sounds (i.e., spellings of sounds) and 2) speech sounds represented by spellings (i.e., pronunciations of spellings). For example, he reports seven spellings for the sound /č/ as in *cello*, *which*, *situation*, etc. and four pronunciations for the spelling *ch* as in *school*, *chaise*, *which*, and *spinach*.

His landmark study, *Relativ frequency of English speech sounds* (revised 1950) was first published by Harvard University Press in 1923. Over the years this publication has become an indispensable reference for scholars concerned with the theoretical aspects of orthography, the teaching of reading and spelling, the psychology of language (speech) and writing (the coding of speech sounds), and communication engineering.

This publication, *Relative frequency of English spellings*, which for comparison is based on the same 100,000 running words used in the previous study, complements Dr. Dewey's first publication on speech sounds. It provides crucial evidence on regularities and irregularities of English spelling with which the reader must cope in decoding writing into speech. On the basis of this evidence, the psychologist can approach word perception in terms of types of learning: category (e.g., *at-cap-mad* versus the *ate-made-cake* categories), cue (e.g., the *ar* of *far* or the *oi* of *noise* cues), and probability (e.g., the likelihood that *ou* will represent the diphthong in *out* rather than the vowel sounds in *soup*, *should*, *country*, *four*, etc.).

In recent years, Dr. Dewey has applied his scholarship to evaluation of initial teaching orthographies, including development of a WES (World English Spelling) version of an initial teaching medium. Some of his conclusions prior to the completion of this study, which have been presented at various international conferences, are cited in the present work, and brought together in a forthcoming companion volume, *English spelling: Roadblock to reading.*

Dr. Dewey's pragmatic approach to the study of phoneme-grapheme relationships supplants opinions with facts. This lucid report of his latest investigation gives the reading "establishment" a scientific basis for research on word perception and offers psycholinguists relevant information for developing adequate theoretical constructs regarding the complexity of the little-understood process called reading. Hence, his report not only is of immediate value but also is a priceless contribution to researchers.

Dr. Godfrey Dewey's record of scholarly production cannot be challenged. His genius has established the hallmarks in orthography, which will serve both scholars and practitioners of the future.

Emmett Albert Betts
Reading Research Laboratory
University of Miami
Coral Gables, Florida

Preface

The purpose of my *Relativ frequency of English speech sounds* (hereafter cited as *RF/Sounds*)[1] was to determine the relative frequency of occurrence, in good English, as written and spoken today, of the various simple sounds and commoner sound combinations—syllables and words—of the English language. Altho first published in 1923, it is still the accepted authority in its particular field. That study, however, did not concern itself with the spellings of the sounds, except insofar as the 1950 revised edition included, as Appendix D, two tables giving the relative frequency of occurrence of the letters of the Roman alphabet, as found in the 100,000 running words investigated.

The purpose of the present study is to determine the relative frequency of each spelling of every sound in representative connected matter; using, in order to facilitate comparison between the data of the phonemic and graphemic studies, the same 100,000 running words investigated in the earlier study. Such data, both phonemic and graphemic, have an immediately important contribution to make to what is increasingly being recognized as the most basic problem of present-day education—*learning to read.* The ability to select for earliest introduction or greatest emphasis, in teaching materials, those phoneme-grapheme correspondences which will occur most frequently *and/or* with the least irregularity is an important aid, regardless of the teaching method employed; more important with the increasing trend toward *code-emphasis* methods rather than

[1] Godfrey Dewey, *Relativ frequency of English speech sounds*, 2nd ed. (Cambridge, Mass.: Harvard University Press, 1950).

meaning-emphasis, recently reported by Chall;[2] and still more important in connection with those code-emphasis methods which employ as an initial teaching medium (hereafter abbreviated to i.t.m.) a substantially phonemic notation, such as Sir James Pitman's Initial Teaching Alphabet, usually referred to as i.t.a.[3]

For the converse educational process, *learning to write*, i.e., to spell, these data supply an important aspect, frequency of occurrence in connected matter, completely missing from the monumental study by Hanna, *et al.*, (hereafter cited as Hanna).[4] Also they provide, for the first time, trustworthy, comprehensive, objective data as a guide for devising or criticizing proposals for reform of English spelling. Their most immediate and important educational contribution, however, is in connection with learning to read.

The practical applications of these data to the immediate problems of learning to read and write English, whether by traditional methods or by the increasingly successful employment of a phonemic notation as an i.t.m., or to the ultimate solution of eliminating the chief obstacles to learning or use of written English by reforming our present English spelling, I have discussed at some length elsewhere.[5] The chief purpose and distinctive contribution of this publication is to provide accurate quantitative objective measurement of the characteristics of our accepted English spelling as it exists today. It is hoped that this study of English graphemes may prove to be, like my earlier study of English phonemes, of important service to other laborers in the educational vineyard.

Acknowledgment is due to Harvard University Press for

[2] Jeanne S. Chall. *Learning to read: The great debate* (New York: McGraw-Hill, 1967).

[3] Sir James Pitman and John St. John, *Alphabets and reading* (New York: Pitman Publishing Corp., 1969), especially Ch. 7, pp. 117–146.

[4] Paul R. Hanna, Jean S. Hanna, Richard E. Hodges, and Edwin H. Rudorf, Jr., *Phoneme-grapheme correspondences as cues to spelling improvement* (Washington, D.C.: U.S. Government Printing Office, 1966 [Doc. OE-32008]).

[5] Godfrey Dewey, *English spelling: Roadblock to reading* (New York: Teachers College Press, in press).

permission to draw freely on the material of my earlier study, *Relativ frequency of English speech sounds*, including reproduction of the substance of Table 4. Also, I am greatly indebted to Dr. Ben D. Wood, whose extraordinary lifetime career as an educational reformer makes him a man after my own heart, for his constant encouragement and helpfulness.

GODFREY DEWEY

Lake Placid Club, N.Y.
October, 1969

Contents

Appendixes

Relative frequency of English spellings

Abbreviations

(with place where first introduced)

RF/Sounds	Dewey, *Relativ frequency of English speech sounds* (Preface, p. v)
i.t.m.	Initial teaching medium (Preface, p. vi)
i.t.a.	Sir James Pitman's Initial Teaching Alphabet (Preface, p. vi)
Hanna	Hanna, *et al.*, *Phoneme-grapheme correspondences* (Preface, p. vi)
T.O.	Traditional orthography (Ch. 1, p. 1)
Hws	Dewey, *How we spell*! (Ch. 1, p. 3)
WNI-3	*Webster's Third New International Dictionary* (Ch. 2, p. 14)
schwi	The high front unstressed vowel (Ch. 2, p. 14)
WES	World English Spelling (Ch. 2, p. 15)
WNI-2	*Webster's Second New International Dictionary* (Ch. 2, p. 19)
x/y	x = number of occurrences, y = number of different items (Ch. 6, p. 87)

Chapter 1

Preliminary discussion

Scope

This study does not concern itself with the evolution of the English language, the spoken word, nor with the somewhat divergent evolution of the written representation of that language, English spelling. There is an abundance of material on both topics, readily available to the linguistic scholar. Neither does it concern itself unduly with the finer shades of difference in the pronunciation of a phoneme, which the professional phonetician delights to distinguish and denote; nor with those alternative spellings which the dictionary records, except to the extent that they actually appear on the average printed page. In spite of the scholar's emphasis on diversity, there *is* a consensus of pronunciation, intensified by world-wide oral communications media, which will be recognized anywhere as "good English," even in areas where the local pronunciation may differ significantly. Also, there is (with due allowance for a relatively few differences between British and American usage, typified by *centre* or *honour*) a substantial consensus of spelling, again intensified by world-wide circulation of printed communications. This study, then, concerns itself chiefly with our traditional orthography (hereafter abbreviated to T.O.), as is; with the phonemes and graphemes of English as commonly understood; more specifically, with the relative frequency with which a particular phoneme is represented by a particular grapheme, *and* with the relative frequency with which a particular grapheme represents a particular phoneme — in other words, with the relative frequency of the spellings of sounds and of the pronunciations of spellings.

Previous investigations

Data regarding the phoneme-grapheme correspondences (to adopt Hanna's term) of English may be determined at three different levels: on a dictionary basis; on the basis of unweighted lists of frequent words; or on a running words basis (connected matter, or weighted word-frequency lists).

At the first level, four studies warrant examination:

Ellis, in his *Plea for Phonetic Spelling*,[1] reported 658 spellings of 42 "sounds" (counting muteness and the vocal murmur, roughly equivalent to schwa, associated with the "syllabic" consonants *l*, *m*, and *n*), or an average of 15.7 spellings per sound. Conversely, he reported 379 different spellings, or an average of 1.7 pronunciations per spelling. These figures were inflated, however, by 104 examples based on proper names (e.g., Cholmondeley or Pontefract for /m/); at least 86 cases of duplicate counting of silent letters (e.g., *straight* both for muteness of *gh* and for *ght* for /t/, *debt* both for *bt* for /t/ and for *eb* for /e/, and both s*igh* and s*ighed* altho *ed* was also counted for /d/); and at least 30 words the spellings and/or pronunciations of which are no longer in current dictionaries (e.g., *hatchel* or *flugleman*). Subjected to the same limitations as my own study, cited below, Ellis's 658 spellings boil down to about 438.

Recently, Pitman,[2] following substantially the same guidelines as exemplified by Ellis above (e.g., duplicate counting of spellings involving silent letters, and inclusion of proper names), has listed 793 "falsely implied dis-relationships between phonemes and characters," i.e., spellings of sounds, for the same 41 phonemes distinguished by my own study, below.

[1] A. J. Ellis, *A plea for phonetic spelling*, 2nd ed. (London: Fred Pitman, Phonetic Depot, 1848).

[2] Pitman, *Alphabets and reading*, Table V, pp. 284–296.

New Spelling,[3] the official statement of the spelling reform proposals of the British Simplified Spelling Society, lists, under each phoneme discussed, the number of words in the dictionary (excluding rare words, foreign words, and proper names) exemplifying each grapheme noted for that phoneme. The number of cases is stated, up to 200 or so; beyond that, the notation is simply "many cases" or "very many cases." This study furnished valuable objective data, previously unavailable, to guide the choice of the most useful grapheme for each phoneme, but these data are nowhere brought together in tabular form, either by phonemes or graphemes.

My own compilation, *How we spell!* (hereafter cited as *Hws*),[4] restricted to spellings and/or pronunciations occurring in a single abridged dictionary,[5] excluding proper names, and avoiding, so far as possible, duplicate counting of the same irregularity, lists 561 spellings of 41 sounds (phonemes), an average of 13.7 spellings per sound; involving 280 different spellings (graphemes), an average of 2.0 pronunciations per spelling. Personally, I regard these severely limited figures as a juster measure of the existing chaos of T.O., and therefore perhaps more impressive, than the considerably larger totals reported by Ellis or Pitman as cited above. The items are listed twice: once under phonemes (spellings of sounds), and again under graphemes (pronunciations of spellings). The latter list is arranged in three groups: single letters, simple digraphs, and all other

[3] Walter Ripman and William Archer (1910); revised by Daniel Jones and Harold Orton (1940, 1948), *New Spelling*, 6th ed. (London: Sir Isaac Pitman & Sons, Ltd., 1948).

[4] Godfrey Dewey, *How we spell! or English heterography* (Lake Placid Club, N.Y.: Lake Placid Club Education Foundation, 1968), with 1969 supplement. The principal tables are reprinted in full as appendixes to Dewey, *English spelling: Roadblock to reading*.

[5] The *American College Dictionary* (New York: Random House, 1966) was selected because, among current abridged dictionaries, its 43-symbol pronunciation key comes nearest to a simple phonemic basis. For *Hws*, this key was further reduced to the 41-phoneme basis of the SSA phonemic alphabet by combining the vowel sounds of *age* and *air*, and the stressed and unstressed vowel sounds of *murmur*.

spellings, to facilitate study of the types of irregularities. This study gives no statistical information as to relative frequency of occurrence, but does give a suggestive approximation by choosing as an example for each spelling one of the commonest words that exemplifies it. Thus, under the phoneme /n/, the examples of *n* as in i*n*, or *nn* as in di*nn*er, clearly suggest that those spellings occur in many common words, whereas *mn* as in *mn*emonic indicates no less clearly that that spelling does not occur in any word commoner than that.

At the second level, by far the most significant data, based on a virtually unweighted list of frequently occurring words, are those of the recent Hanna study, previously cited. This study examined exhaustively, using computer techniques, the spelling of every phoneme of 17,310 common words, derived chiefly from the Thorndike-Lorge list (based on a count of some 4½ million running words),[6] taking into account the position of the phoneme (initial, medial, or final) in the syllable, and the degree of stress (primary, secondary, or none). Unfortunately the Thorndike-Lorge list weights only the infrequent words. Its AA category of 1,069 words occurring 100 or more times per million, which, judging from my *RF/Sounds* should make up at least 78% of all writing, includes, without discrimination, words ranging in frequency from *the*, with a probable frequency of some 73,000 words per million, down to words like *winter*, with a probable frequency of about 100 per million; and its A category of 952 words occurring 50 to 99 times per million, which should make up at least an additional 7% of all writing, again makes no discrimination between frequencies within that range. Only for the 15,000 words, more or less, which make up the remaining 15% of most writing (the least trustworthy as well as the least significant portion of the list) are frequencies, ranging from 49 to 1 per million, given. It is therefore impossible to extract from the Hanna study, by any manipulation of data whatsoever, significant information on the relative frequency of occurrence of the

[6] Edward L. Thorndike and Irving Lorge, *The teacher's word book of 30,000 words* (New York: Teachers College Press, 1944).

reported phoneme-grapheme correspondences — such information as it is the primary purpose of the present study to provide. All statistical data in the Hanna study are therefore necessarily expressed only in terms of *items;* that is, the number of different words or syllables involved, without distinction as to their relative importance.

Using these data, and taking into account further so-called environmental factors and the morphological factors of compounding, affixation, and word families, the Hanna study then constructed an algorithm or rule of procedure which manipulated 77 different graphemes according to 203 rules. A computer programmed according to this algorithm was able to spell just under 50% of the investigated 17,310 words correctly, and another 36% with only one error! One could hardly ask for a better or more objective measure of the burden which spelling reform seeks to lift from elementary education than the foregoing figures.

The Hanna study depended on Merriam-Webster's *New Collegiate Dictionary*, 6th edition, as its authority for pronunciations, but reduced the 62 symbols there distinguished to 52, which is still too many for the general public to discriminate. On the 52-phoneme basis reported, Hanna (Tables 7 and 8) found 378 phoneme-grapheme correspondences or spellings, involving a total of 170 different graphemes. Reducing these figures, however, to the 41-phoneme basis of this study, *RF/Sounds*, and *Hws*, Hanna's findings become 325 spellings, involving 160 different graphemes. Other comparisons with my own data will be made at appropriate points in later chapters.

Since the chief purpose of the Hanna study was to provide trustworthy objective data as a guide to the teaching of *spelling*, his results are presented in terms of the spellings of sounds, disregarding the converse aspect of the pronunciations of spellings, which is of at least comparable importance for the teaching of reading. To bring out this latter aspect, I have, in Appendix A, restated the data of Hanna's Tables 7 and 8 in terms of grapheme-phoneme correspondences; that is, pronunciations of spellings. The graphemes are grouped by single letters, simple digraphs, and all other spellings, as in *Hws*, and the phonemes are arranged under each grapheme in the order of frequency of *items*, the only frequency information available. To facilitate comparison both with Hanna and the present study, the phonemes are denoted not only by the arbitrary Hanna code of numbered capital letters, necessitated by the limitations of computer print-outs, but also by the more immediately intelligible symbols of the Simpler Spelling Association (SSA) phonemic alphabet employed in this study, presented and discussed in the next chapter.

Materials and methods

For the corpus of the present study there were available the original data cards for each of the 10,119 different words of the 100,000 running words of my previous *RF/Sounds* study; each card showing, on the top line, the frequency of occurrence, the word itself in dictionary spelling, with the number of letters (not used in the present investigation), the word respelled, showing syllable divisions, in the 48-phoneme Revised Scientific Alphabet used as Key 1 in the Funk & Wagnalls *New Standard Dictionary* current in 1918, and the number of phonemes and syllables (again, not used in the present investigation).

Since conversion of these original cards to machine-readable form, incidentally involving some arbitrary letter-plus-figure code for the print-outs, would have required at least as much labor as the analysis itself and would have introduced the possibility of errors in the conversion, the same technique employed for the original study, using rubber stamps and specially ruled cards, was again employed. A separate card was set up for each grapheme for each phoneme (8 different cards, for example, for the grapheme *a*; one for each phoneme which it represented), and the word frequency was entered by rubber stamp for each phoneme of every word, distinguishing by column rulings whether the phoneme was initial, medial, final, or alone in its syllable, and supplying additional cards as the columns filled with entries. Some of the most regular spellings of the most frequent sounds, such as *r* for /r/, required over 5,000 separate entries on 50-odd cards, which eventually were cumulated on a single card for each phoneme-grapheme correspondence. The full information thus secured, on the 48-phoneme basis, was then compiled in Appendix C, from which the other tables were derived by the consolidations necessary to present the principal data of the study on the broader 41-phoneme basis, more useful to the average layman without specific phonetic training, whether student or teacher, as distinct from the professional linguist.

The phonemic basis for this study, including the notation employed, is discussed in Chapter 2. The graphemic basis employed to assure consistent assignment of letters to spellings and avoid duplicate counting of the same irregularity, such as was done deliberately by Ellis and Pitman, is discussed in Chapter 3.

Chapter 2

Phonemic basis

At the professional level of linguistic scholarship, there are wide divergencies of opinion both as to the number and nature of the sounds of English speech and as to the notation to be employed to denote those characteristics. At one time the alphabet of the International Phonetic Association (IPA) seemed to offer an acceptable standard, yet as used by Kenyon in his *Pronouncing Dictionary of American English*,[1] it differs substantially from the form used by Daniel Jones, who with Paul Passy founded the IPA and was for many years its guiding genius, in his *English Pronouncing Dictionary*;[2] and more recent innovators, insofar as they pay lip service to the IPA alphabet at all, do so by describing their own notation as a modification thereof. For the professional phonetician or linguist, their more subtle distinctions and analyses are no doubt valuable, and their more complex notations a useful tool of scholarship, but for the general public, untrained in phonetics, such sophistications present a repellent and almost insurmountable barrier. Fortunately we need not concern ourselves here with these subtleties, for whereas the purposes of the linguistic scholar are best served by a phonetic notation of *maximum* precision, which seeks to symbolize every discernible shade of difference in the sounds of English speech, the purposes of this study, which should have its chief impact at the elemen-

[1] John S. Kenyon, and Thomas A. Knott, *A pronouncing dictionary of American English* (Springfield, Mass.: G. & C. Merriam Co., 1944).

[2] Daniel Jones, *Everyman's English pronouncing dictionary*, 11th ed. (London: J. M. Dent & Sons, Ltd., 1957).

tary school level and with the general public wholly unversed in phonetics, will best be served by a *phonemic* notation of *minimum* precision; that is, a notation making those distinctions, and only those distinctions, which are semantically significant, and making only those distinctions readily recognizable by the average untrained ear. Incidentally, such a notation will be broad enough to absorb the most important regional differences, as well as to wash out most of the controversial sophistications of the phonetic level.

The one phonemic code for writing English which has been proved in practical experience by millions of writers for more than a century is the 40-sound basis of Pitmanic shorthand; commonly classed as 24 consonants, 12 vowels, and 4 diphthongs, disregarding such sophistications as whether the vowel sounds of *bait* or *boat* are in fact diphthongs, or whether the "vowel" sounds of *youth* and *few* are different or the same, and if the same, whether they are both consonant plus vowel or both true diphthongs. These 40 sounds are also the phonemic basis, with slight modifications of the graphemic treatment, of Pitman's i.t.a., which is being used with conspicuous success in the first teaching of reading and writing, both in this country and Great Britain as well as the other English-speaking countries, and, with slight further modifications, for the teaching of English as a second language in a number of non-English-speaking countries.

The Simpler Spelling Association (SSA) phonemic alphabet, shown in Table 1, in which most of the results of this study are stated, agrees precisely with the foregoing 40-sound basis except for two details: 1) Addition of the internationally accepted symbol for the low or mid-central vowel sound known as schwa, /ə/; 2) Its distinctive treatment of the definite article, *the*, as a single speech unit or "phoneme." This alphabet is a direct evolution from the 1877 "Standard Fonetic Alfabet" of the American Philological Association,[3] which was reworked by committees of the

[3] Francis A. March, *The spelling reform* (Washington: Bureau of Education, 1893), Circular of Information, No. 8, pp. 17–21.

Table 1 SSA Phonemic Alphabet

24 consonants

Character: Lower case	Character: Capital	*Name*	As in
p	**p**	*pə*	**p**in, cu**p**
b	**b**	*bə*	**b**in, cu**b**
t	**t**	*tə*	**t**en, be**t**
d	**d**	*də*	**d**en, be**d**
k	**k**	*kə*	**c**ome, ba**ck**
g	**g**	*gə*	**g**um, ba**g**
f	**f**	*fə*	**f**an, sa**f**e
v	**v**	*və*	**v**an, sa**v**e
ꜧ	**ꜧ**	*ꜧə*	**th**igh, ba**th**
ħ	**ħ**	*ħə*	**th**y, ba**the**
s	**s**	*sə*	**s**eal, ra**c**e
z	**z**	*zə*	**z**eal, rai**s**e
ʃ	**ʃ**	*ʃə*	a**ss**ure, ru**sh**
ʒ	**ʒ**	*ʒə*	a**z**ure, rou**g**e
ƈ	**ƈ**	*ƈə*	**ch**oke, ri**ch**
j	**j**	*jə*	**j**oke, ri**dge**
m	**m**	*mə*	**m**et, hi**m**
n	**n**	*nə*	**n**et, thi**n**
ŋ	**ŋ**	*vŋ*	i**n**k, thi**ng**
l	**l**	*lə*	**l**aid, dea**l**
r	**r**	*rə*	**r**aid, dea**r**
w	**w**	*wə*	**w**et, **w**e
y	**y**	*yə*	**y**et, **y**e
h	**h**	*hə*	**h**ead, **h**e

13 vowels

Character: Lower case	Character: Capital	*Name*	As in
a	**a**	*ak*	**a**m, p**a**t
ɑ	**ɑ**	*ɑ*	**a**lms, p**a**rt, m**a**
e	**e**	*ek*	**e**dge, l**e**t
ɐ	**ɐ**	*ɐ*	**a**ge, l**a**te, m**ay**; **air**
i	**i**	*ik*	**i**s, s**i**t, arm**y**
ε	**ε**	*ε*	**ea**se, s**ea**t, m**e**
ɒ	**ɒ**	*ɒk*	**o**dd, n**o**t
ɔ	**ɔ**	*ɔ*	**aw**ed, n**augh**t, psh**aw**
ʊ	**ʊ**	*ʊk*	**u**p, t**o**n
o	**o**	*o*	**o**pen, t**o**ne, sh**ow**
u	**u**	*uk*	f**u**ll, sh**ou**ld
ɯ	**ɯ**	*ɯ*	f**oo**l, sh**oe**d, sh**oe**
ə	**ə**	*ər*	**a**bout, m**ur**m**ur**, dat**a**

4 diphthongs

Character: Lower case	Character: Capital	*Name*	As in
ȧ	**ȧ**	*ȧ*	**ai**sle, p**i**nt, b**y**
ɑu	**ɑu**	*ɑu*	**ow**l, p**ou**nd, b**ough**
ɔ̇	**ɔ̇**	*ɔ̇*	**oi**l, p**oi**nt, b**oy**
ɯ̇	**ɯ̇**	*ɯ̇*	**u**sed, p**u**re, d**ue**

Supplementary signs

Character: Lower case	Character: Capital	*Name*	As in
ƀ	**ƀ**	*ƀ*	**the** (wordsign)
*	*	*capsign*	

To capitalize a typewritten or longhand word, write the capsign before it.

Phonemic print capitals are heavy or boldface letters, otherwise similar to the small or lower-case letters.

liŋkən'z getizbərg adres

forskor and sevn yɛrz əgo ɑır fɑħərz brɔt forɧ ɒn ħis kɒntinənt ə niɯ nɑʃən, kənsɛvd in libərti, and dedikɑted tu ħə prɒpəziʃən ħat ɔl men ɑr krɛɑted ɛkwəl.

nɑı wɛ ɑr engɑjd in ə grɑt sivil wɔr, testiŋ hweħər ħat nɑʃən, ɔr eni nɑʃən so kənsɛvd and so dedikɑted, kan lɔŋ endiɯr. **w**ɛ ɑr met ɒn ə grɑt batl-fɛld ɒv ħat wɔr. **w**ɛ hav kum tu dedikɑt ə porʃən ɒv ħat fɛld az ə fánəl restiŋ-plɑs fɔr ħoz hɯ hɛr gɑv ħɑr lávz ħat ħat nɑʃən mát liv. **i**t iz ɔltəgeħər fitiŋ and prɒpər ħat wɛ ʃud dɯ ħis.

but in ə lɑrjər sens, wɛ kanɒt dedikɑt — wɛ kanɒt kɒnsikrɑt — wɛ kanɒt halo — ħis grɑınd. **ħə** brɑv men, liviŋ and ded, hɯ strugld hɛr, hav kɒnsikrɑted it fɑr əbuv ɑır pɯr pɑıər tu ad ɔr ditrakt. **ħə** wərld wil litl not nɔr lɔŋ rimembər hwɒt wɛ sɑ hɛr, but it kan nevər fərget hwɒt ħɑ did hɛr. **i**t iz fɔr us, ħə liviŋ, raħər, tu bɛ dedikɑted hɛr tu ħə unfiniʃt wərk hwić ħɑ hɯ fɔt hɛr hav ħus fɑr so nobli ədvanst. **i**t iz raħər fɔr us tu bɛ hɛr dedikɑted tu ħə grɑt task rimɑniŋ bifor us — ħat frɒm ħɛz ɒnərd ded wɛ tɑk inkrɛst divoʃən tu ħat kɔz fɔr hwić ħɑ gɑv ħə last ful meʒər ɒv divoʃən; ħat wɛ hɛr háli rizɒlv ħat ħɛz ded ʃal nɒt hav dád in vɑn; ħat ħis nɑʃən, undər **g**ɒd, ʃal hav ə niɯ bərɧ ɒv frɛdəm; and ħat guvərnmənt ɒv ħə pɛpl, bá ħə pɛpl, fɔr ħə pɛpl, ʃal nɒt periʃ frɒm ħə ərɧ.

Brief study of the preceding page will enable anyone to read the above selection accurately. A few hours of study will give anyone at all familiar with phonetics a practical working knowledge of this simple and suitable phonemic alphabet for English.

Department of Superintendence of the National Education Association, the American Philological Association, and the Modern Language Association between 1904 and 1911 to produce the Revised Scientific Alphabet, popularly known as the NEA alphabet.[4] This 48-phoneme alphabet was used as Key 1 of the Funk & Wagnalls *New Standard Dictionaries* of that period, which, for that reason, I selected as the authority for the basic research of my *RF/Sounds*, and, in consequence, of the present study.

The Simplified Spelling Board (SSB) "Fonetic Key Alfabet," in which most of the results of my *RF/Sounds* study were presented,[5] was a reduction of the 48-phoneme NEA alphabet, devised primarily for dictionary key purposes, to the 41-phoneme basis deemed more suitable for general popular use. In making this reduction, the committee of the SSB sought to minimize the departures from the NEA alphabet: retaining at least two symbols for which they felt the IPA symbols were clearly preferable; retaining the macron (slightly curved to suggest a circumflex, to minimize confusion with the predominant "Webster" usage of the macron for the name-sounds of the vowels); and making two combinations, clearly suggested by the NEA symbols, with which some members of the committee, including myself, disagreed.

The Spelling Reform Association (SRA) "Fonetic Alfabet," an interim stage of evolution, was a 1928 revision of the 1922 SSB alphabet by a committee consisting of the principal officers of the SSB and SRA, in association with Frederic W. Goudy, the foremost type designer of his generation. Its chief purpose was to achieve maximum congruity with the existing lower-case letters of the Roman alphabet, including so far as possible the elimination of diacritics. Mr. Goudy contributed nothing to the phonemic aspect, which indeed remained virtually unchanged, but the committee adopted no new character until he had produced

[4] Raymond Weeks, James W. Bright, Charles H. Grandgent, *The N.E.A. Phonetic Alphabet: with a review of the Whipple experiments* (Lancaster, Pa.: New Era Printing Co., 1912), pp. 6–10.

[5] See *RF/Sounds*, Appendix A, pp. 135–138.

a working drawing which he was willing to pass as conforming to the canons of design of the lower-case Roman alphabet. In consequence, the present SSA alphabet, shown in Table 1, which involves only a couple of minor changes (chiefly elimination of a special symbol for the vowel of *air*), is, I believe, more compatible with T.O. than any other one sign, one sound phonemic notation of comparable validity. Table 1 includes a familiar specimen of connected matter which exemplifies this essentially "self-reading" compatibility, at the same time that it gives the reader unfamiliar with this particular phonemic notation practice in recognizing the symbols.

The special treatment of the definite article, *the*, by a single symbol, introduced as far back as the 1922 SSB alphabet used in *RF/Sounds*, is for two reasons: 1) *The* has three pronunciations concurrently in good usage: /ħε/, emphatic (the least frequent); /ħi/, before a vowel (and sometimes before /h/); and /ħə/, unemphatic, before a consonant; and no practical system of transcription at the phonemic level should consider writing a common word in three different ways. 2) Considered as a single "phoneme," *the* occurs more frequently than over half of the 41 true phonemes, so that the economy of effort achieved by a single symbol is substantial; also, whatever arbitrary assumptions may be made as to the relative frequency of each of the three pronunciations will be large enough to distort seriously the figures for the known frequencies of the three vowels involved. For the purpose of *RF/Sounds*, Table 15, the only 48-phoneme data in that study, these assumptions were: /ħε/, 10%; /ħi/, 30%; and /ħə/, 60%; and to facilitate comparison the same assumptions were carried over for Appendix C, the only 48-phoneme data of this study. Similarly, the assumption that the indefinite article *a* was pronounced 10% stressed /ɑ/, and 90% unstressed /ə/, was carried over for Appendix C.

The reductions made to convert the 48-phoneme raw data to the more serviceable 41-phoneme (plus *the*) basis of the SSA phonemic alphabet eliminated the following 7 distinctions:

1. Between the stressed /**ɑ**/ of *art* and the unstressed /**ɑ**/ of *artistic*

2. Between the stressed /**ō**/ of *open* and the unstressed /**o**/ of *obey*

3. Between the stressed /**iū**/ of *feud* and the unstressed /**iu**/ of *futility*

4. Between the stressed /**ʊ**/ and the unstressed /**ə**/ of *murmur*

5. Between the stressed /**i**/ and the unstressed /**ı**/ of *pity*

6. Between the vowel sounds of *aim* and *air*

7. The ambivalent symbol for the variant pronunciations of *ask*

The first three of these combinations are sufficiently obvious, and their unimportance is further emphasized by the infrequent occurrence of the unstressed forms: /ɑ/, .02%; /o/, .33%; /iu/, .02%. The fourth is the treatment of schwa, /ə/, which I urged in *RF/Sounds* but did not feel free to adopt at that time, but which is now adopted by *Webster's Third New International Dictionary* (WNI-3) and the corresponding *Webster's Seventh New Collegiate Dictionary*. In passing, I emphatically *disagree* with the additional use of this schwa symbol by WNI-3 for the stressed vowel of *but* (where no following /r/ is involved), which I regard as a quite distinct phoneme — a position with which both Kenyon[6] and Jones,[7] as well as Kurath[8] and others, agree.

The fifth reduction eliminates, for popular use, a special symbol for the high front unstressed vowel, which Sir James Pitman has aptly named "schwi" (the undotted *i* of the NEA alphabet, the barred or crossed *i* of some more recent notations), which combines most of the shortness of /i/

[6] Kenyon, *Pronouncing dictionary*, p. xvii and note 19 on p. xx.

[7] Daniel Jones, *An outline of English phonetics*, 8th ed. (Cambridge, England: W. Heffer & Sons, Ltd., 1957), pp. 86–88.

[8] Hans Kurath, *A phonology and prosody of modern English* (Ann Arbor: University of Michigan Press, 1967), pp. 93–95.

with much of the closeness of /ɛ/. Both Kenyon[9] and Jones[10] find a separate symbol for this phoneme, as distinct from the "short *i*" of *bit*, unnecessary, and use their respective "short *i*" symbols for the unstressed final vowel of *pity* as well as for the preceding stressed vowel. Use of a symbol for schwi, in a dictionary key to pronunciation, would, however, avoid such deplorable consequences as the use by WNI-3 of their "long e" symbol, with its inescapable suggestion of some degree of stress, for this unstressed final vowel, instead of the "short i" symbol used in their preceding editions and in most current dictionaries. As it is, they key *trusty* and *trustee* exactly alike except for the stress marks, which, of course do not carry over into ordinary writing.

The sixth reduction, combining the vowel of *air* with the vowel of *aim*, agrees with the century-old practice of Pitmanic shorthand and the current practice of i.t.a., as well as with the New Spelling of the British Simplified Spelling Society and the World English Spelling, usually referred to as WES, of the Simpler Spelling Association. Phoneticians in general tend to regard this phoneme as closer to the vowel of *bat* or of *bet* rather than *bait;* but the SRA alphabet included for several years a separate symbol for the *air* vowel, which most of the committee members regarded as quite unessential at that level, because the two top phoneticians of the committee could not agree as to whether combining it with /a/ or with /e/ was preferable! The untrained ear, however, more readily accepts /ɑ/ as the nearest equivalent. This is one of several cases where a following /r/ exerts a marked influence on a preceding vowel, whether the unmodified vowel be considered as having been long or short. A parallel case is the vowel of *here*, which most current dictionaries denote as short, whereas the layman accepts more readily the treatment with the long vowel, as in the Funk & Wagnalls dictionary used for

[9] Kenyon, *Pronouncing dictionary*, p. xvii and note 6 on p. xviii.

[10] Jones, *English pronouncing dictionary*, 2nd cover and p. xlii, and very many examples thruout the vocabulary.

Table 2 Reconciliation of:

Revised Scientific Alphabet (RSA), 48 phonemes —
employed for primary analysis of 100,000-word corpus of both frequency studies

Simplified Spelling Board (SSB) Fonetic Key Alfabet, 41 phonemes-plus-*the* —
employed for most tables of syllables and sounds in *RF/Sounds*

Simpler Spelling Association (SSA) Phonemic Alphabet, 41 phonemes-plus-*the* —
employed in most tables (all but Appendixes A, B, and C) in this study

Consonants

As in	RSA 48 phonemes	SSB 41 phonemes	SSA 41 phonemes
*p*in, cu*p*	**p**	—	—
*b*in, cu*b*	**b**	—	—
*t*en, be*t*	**t**	—	—
*d*en, be*d*	**d**	—	—
*c*ome, ba*ck*	**k**	—	—
*g*um, ba*g*	**g**	—	—
*f*an, sa*f*e	**f**	—	—
*v*an, sa*v*e	**v**	—	—
*th*igh, ba*th*, *th*in	**th**	**ħ**	**ꜧ**
*th*y, ba*the*, *th*is	**th**	**đ**	**ħ** (8)
*s*eal, ra*c*e	**s**	—	—
*z*eal, rai*s*e	**z**	—	—
*sh*all, as*s*ure, ru*sh*	**sh**	**ʃ**	—
*j*abot, a*z*ure, rou*g*e	**ʒ**	—	—
*ch*oke, ri*ch*, *ch*ur*ch*	**ch**	**ç**	**ƈ**
*j*oke, ri*dg*e, *j*u*dg*e	**j**	—	—
*m*et, hi*m*	**m**	—	—
*n*et, thi*n*	**n**	—	—
i*n*k, thi*ng*	**ŋ**	—	—
*l*aid, dea*l*	**l**	—	—
*r*aid, dea*r*	**r**	—	—
*w*et, *w*e	**w**	—	—
*y*et, *y*e	**y**	—	—
*h*ead, *h*e	**h**	—	—

Vowels

As in	RSA	SSB	SSA
*a*m, p*a*t	**a**	**a** (1)	**a** (9)
*a*ir, c*a*re, th*e*re	**ā** *		
*a*sk, f*a*st, p*a*th	**ɑ** *		

As in	RSA 48 phonemes	SSB 41 phonemes	SSA 41 phonemes
*a*rtistic, c*a*rtoon	ɑ	ɑ (2)	
*a*rt, *a*lms, f*a*ther	ɑ̄ *		
*e*dge, l*e*t	e	—	—
*a*ge, l*a*te, m*ay*	ē	ê	ɞ (10)
an*y*, hab*i*t, cit*ie*s	ɪ *		
*i*s, s*i*t	i	i (3)	—
*ea*se, s*ea*t, m*e*	ɪ̄	ɪ̂	ɛ
*o*dd, n*o*t, w*a*s	ɵ	—	ɒ
*o*r, h*au*l, psh*aw*	ɵ̄	ɵ̂	ɔ
*u*p, t*o*n, b*u*t	ʊ	ʊ (4)	ʊ (11)
b*ur*n, h*er*, f*ir*st, w*or*k	ʊ̄ *		
*a*bout, ov*er*, dat*a*	ə	ə (5)	ə (12)
*o*bey, p*o*etic, wind*ow*	o	o (6)	—
*o*pen, n*o*te, sh*ow*	ō *		
f*u*ll, g*oo*d, sh*ou*ld	u	—	—
f*oo*l, f*oo*d, sh*oe*	ū	û	ɯ

Diphthongs

*ai*sle, p*i*nt, b*y*	ɑi	ȧ	—
*oi*l, p*oi*nt, b*oy*	ɵi	ɵ̇	ɔ̇
*ow*l, p*ou*nd, b*ough*	ɑu	ɑı	—
d*u*ration, f*u*tility	iu	u̇ (7)	ɯ̇
p*u*re, f*eu*d, b*eau*ty	iū *		

Wordsign

the	(thī, thɪ, thə) **	ŧī	ŧə

Notes

* RSA symbol eliminated in SSB and SSA alphabets

** Dictionaries give three pronunciations. Wordsign in SSB and SSA

— Same form and signification as symbol at left

(1) Includes ȧ (*ai*r) and a (*a*sk) (2) Includes ɑ̄ (*a*rt)

(3) Includes high front unstressed vowel "schwi" ɪ (an*y*)

(4) Includes ʊ̄ (b*ur*n)

(5) Includes only unstressed schwa ə (*a*bout)

(6) Includes ō (*o*pen) (7) Includes iū (p*u*re)

(8) Represents *voiced*, not unvoiced, *th*

(9) Includes vowel of *a*sk, but not vowel of *ai*r

(10) Represents vowel of *a*ge, including vowel of *ai*r

(11) Includes only vowel of b*u*t, not including stressed schwa of b*ur*n

(12) Includes both unstressed schwa of ov*er* and stressed schwa of b*ur*n

RF/Sounds. The WNI-3 transcription, with a parenthetic /ə/ following the short vowel, appears quite needlessly sophisticated for general use.

Finally, the seventh reduction merely eliminates the ambivalent symbol employed in a dictionary key to avoid printing both accepted variants of the *ask* vowel, /ask/ or /ɑsk/, wherever they occur.

Note at this point that any different combination (or separation) of phonemes, for whatever purpose, within the limits of the Revised Scientific Alphabet, may readily be derived from Appendix C, which gives the complete data obtained on a 48-phoneme basis. Table 2, with its notes, exhibits a complete reconciliation of the three notations employed, for reasons explained above, in *RF/Sounds* and in this study.

I am well aware that the particular 41-phoneme classification adopted for *RF/Sounds* and for this study will be a target for criticism by those more sophisticated linguists who prefer to treat all or most of the long vowels as diphthongs or glides, or what have you, and make other subtle distinctions appropriate and perhaps valuable for discussion among linguistic scholars but baffling to the point of complete unintelligibility for the general public. The decisions involved have been based not only on the historical background of experience cited above but also on some seventy years of personal experience in writing English phonemically, whether in shorthand or longhand, on a substantially 40-sound basis, and teaching others to write similarly, especially in shorthand; as well as nearly fifty years of active concern with the problems of spelling reform, including several items of research, and service on various committees, both here and abroad, concerned with devising, or more often revising, phonemic notations, whether as teaching instruments or for spelling reform. In my considered judgment, this particular phonemic classification represents the maximum, and probably the optimum, degree of discrimination with which the general public can learn to deal effectively.

A word of explanation to assist in relating to the present study the findings of the Hanna study, which relied on the preposterous[11] Merriam-Webster key to pronunciation, which was used virtually unchanged in *Webster's Second New International Dictionary* (WNI-2) and its principal abridgments for 50 years. Hanna reduced the 62 symbols of that key — which employed for the one phoneme which WNI-3 now recognizes as schwa 6 regular symbols (with 4 additional alternative symbols suggested) for the unstressed occurrences, with a 7th (or 11th) for the stressed occurrences — to his 52 symbols, by combinations similar in principle to the reductions of the NEA alphabet noted above. These 10 are sufficiently explained by comparing his Table 3 and Table 2; and it is suggested later in his text (pp. 122–123) that he might well have carried these reductions even further.

Reduction of the Hanna 52-phoneme basis to the 41-phoneme basis of this study involves:

Eliminating the three symbols, /HW/, /KS/, and /KW/, which represent consonant clusters, not single phonemes.

Eliminating the distinctions between /L1/, /M1/, and /N1/ for the "syllabic" consonants, commonly regarded today as preceded by at least a vestigial schwa, and /L/, /M/, and /N/.

These 6, together with Hanna's /H9/ symbol for the silent *h* of *honest* (listed but not counted in his 52), discussed in the next chapter, were kept track of in this study by *duplicate* entries which did not disturb the primary analysis, and are listed, for comparison with Hanna's findings, as Appendix B.

Also eliminated are 5 additional vowel distinctions, sufficiently explained in the heading to Appendix A, which reconciles the Hanna vowel notation with the SSA alphabet.

[11] Weeks *et al.*, *The N.E.A. Phonetic Alphabet.* Pages 10–19 contain a scathing indictment of the Webster key, fully warranted by the circumstances under which it was written.

Chapter 3

Graphemic basis

The problem of the graphemic basis is simply to assure the most logical and consistent assignment of letters to the spelling of each phoneme, and at the same time to avoid counting the same irregularity twice, as was done deliberately by Ellis and Pitman (*vide supra*, Ch. 1, p. 2). The "Delimitation of spellings" employed for *Hws*, reproduced below, together with the third paragraph of the "Arrangement of spellings table," which explains the notation for certain irregularities, served as the guide for this study, except where differences in the dictionaries on which each was based necessitated slight modifications or where unforeseen subtleties required one or two supplementary notes.

Delimitation of spellings

These tables are limited to spellings and/or pronunciations occurring in the *American College Dictionary*,[1] which contains about 132,000 words (71,000 main entries); less than 30% of the 450,000 words in the best-known unabridged dictionary. Also, no proper names, however common, have been included.

To maintain a measure of consistency and eliminate duplicate counting of silent letters, *all consonant letters* except the semi-vowels *w*, *y*, and *h have been treated as part of the spelling of a consonant sound*, and *all vowel letters have been treated as part of the spelling of a vowel sound*, with only four exceptions:

[1] See note 5, Ch. 1

Where their position in a word renders such treatment impossible; e.g., ch*o*ir, q*u*ite, throu*gh*, depo*t*.

Where the silent letters *gh* follow a long vowel; e.g., str*aigh*t /ɑ/, m*igh*t /ȧ/, c*augh*t /ɔ/, b*ough*t /ɔ/.

In some spellings of /ʃ/, /ʒ/, /č/, and /j/, where linguistically the grapheme for the consonant phoneme is considered to include a following *i* or *e*; e.g., na*ti*on, oc*e*an, mi*ssi*on, vi*si*on, ques*ti*on, sol*di*er.

In the suffix *-ed*, when pronounced /t/ or /d/; e.g., ask*ed*, call*ed*.

Arrangement of spellings table

This table lists only the spellings of single sounds: therefore, where one letter, such as *x* in ne*x*t, represents two sounds, or two letters taken together, such as *oi* in mem*oi*r, represent two sounds each quite different from the normal value of the separate letter, or in a different order, as with the letters *wh* for the sounds /hw/, each of the separate sounds has been listed as spelled by ½ of the combination; e.g., *½x* as a spelling of /k/ and *½x* as a spelling of /s/, etc.

The first edition of *Hws*[2] confined its definition of spellings to the single concept of consonants (except for *y*) as part of a consonant spelling, vowels as part of a vowel spelling, altho not counting *-ed* as a spelling of /d/ or /t/ resulted in an unwarrantable number of vowel spellings of the form vowel-(consonant)-silent e.

The second edition[3] continued the above treatment of *-ed*, recognizing *y* as sometimes to be regarded as part of a vowel spelling, and recognized further (without, however, changing the rules) that in some words such as *soldier*, *gingham*, or *knowledge*, a different treatment would be obviously more etymologic.

[2] Godfrey Dewey, *How we spel: or English heterografy* (Cambridge, Mass.: Simplified Spelling Board, 1923).

[3] Godfrey Dewey, *English heterografy: or How we spel* (Lake Placid Club, N.Y.: Lake Placid Club Education Foundation, 1963).

The further changes in the current edition (1968) reflected in the "Delimitation of spellings" above were made with the twofold purpose of conforming more closely to etymology and morphology without sacrificing the safeguards against duplicate counting, and of coming as close as could be justified to the decisions governing the graphemic aspect of the Hanna study. Decisions forced on the Hanna study by the limitations of computer technique were, of course, avoided. In particular, his graphemic symbol, /H9/, for the silent *h* of *honest*, etc., listed but not counted as one of his 52 phonemes, was rejected in favor of distributing these "silent *h*" spellings with the associated vowels with which they rightly belong; for it must be obvious that since *honest* would be misspelled if it lacked the initial *h*, and since the *h* cannot possibly be considered to be a part of the /n/, /e/, /s/, or /t/ phoneme, it must be regarded as part of the spelling of the /ɒ/ phoneme, just as the silent *t* at the end of depo*t* must be regarded as part of the spelling of the /o/ phoneme.

The two supplementary guidelines below were formulated to assure uniformity of treatment of final or semi-final vowels, especially in connection with syllabic consonants, which were recognized by the WNI-2 notation of the dictionary employed by Hanna, and by the dictionary on which the 48-phoneme data of *RF/Sounds* and the present Appendix C are based, but not by the dictionary on which *Hws* is based nor by the normal usage of the SSA phonemic alphabet.

1. *Associate a final or semi-final vowel with its root word, so far as possible.* Thus the grapheme for /ɑ/ is *a-e*, both in *grade* and *grades*, but *a* in *graded*, because the semi-final /e/ must be regarded as the only possible spelling for the /e/ in *ed*. Likewise the grapheme for the syllabic /n/ of *taken* is *n*, not *en;* because the *e* is already associated with the grapheme *a-e* for the /ɑ/ of the root word.

2. *Except as above, associate a vowel immediately preceding syllabic /n/, or preceding or following syllabic /l/, with its syllable.* Thus the grapheme for syllabic /n/ in *sudden* is *en;* for syllabic /l/ in *evil* is *il;* for syllabic /l/ in *people* is *le*. This latter example differs from *Hws*, where the dictionary

phonemic transcription is /pɛpəl/, and the spelling for the final /l/ is therefore given as *½le*.

All but 22 of the 397 spellings reported in Appendix C appear in the current edition of *Hws*, which is readily available.[4] The missing 22 examples are reported in Appendix D. As there noted, 7 are due to the different treatment of syllabic consonants noted above; 11 are due to different treatment of /yu/ and /iu/, on which no two of the six dictionaries referred to in this study agree completely; and 4 to other slight difference between the respective dictionaries.

[4] See note 4, Ch. 1.

Chapter 4

Spellings of sounds (Phoneme-grapheme correspondences)

The principal data of this study are reported in Table 5, Spellings of sounds, and Table 6, Pronunciations of spellings. These data, as there presented and summarized, speak for themselves, but since their substance will be relatively unfamiliar to most readers, a few additional comments and supplementary tables may help to place the data in perspective.

I have accepted provisionally, with some misgivings, Hanna's term, "phoneme-grapheme correspondences," to signify the category which I have termed in *Hws*, "spellings of sounds." His term carries with it, by implication, the term, "grapheme-phoneme correspondences," for the category which I have termed, "pronunciations of spellings," with which the Hanna study does not deal. Obviously, the first category is important chiefly for writing, i.e., spelling; the second chiefly for reading. For the interrelationship, without regard to which category is implied, I have, in general, used the first designation, "phoneme-grapheme correspondences."

The relative frequency of occurrence of a particular phoneme-grapheme correspondence on the printed page is obviously a product of two factors: the relative frequency of the phoneme itself, and the proportion of its occurrences represented by that particular grapheme. For ready reference in connection with the first factor, Table 3 presents the 41 phonemes plus *the* (*vide supra*, Ch. 2, p. 13) in order of frequency of occurrences, together with the number of spellings of each found in this study. This table is not strictly comparable with *RF/Sounds*, Table 17, its nearest equivalent, for two reasons: 1) This study combines the vowel of *air* with the vowel of *aim*, and the stressed occurrences of schwa with the unstressed, whereas *RF/Sounds*, for reasons explained in Chapter 2, combined the *air* and *at* vowels, and combined stressed schwa with the vowel of *but*. 2) In repeating the analysis of phonemes after 50 years, with different help and a somewhat different emphasis, it was inevitable that individual items, some of which involved as many as 5,000 separate entries, would not check out exactly. The over-all discrepancy, both in occurrences and items, is less than 0.3%, not enough to affect the practical significance of any findings, and most individual variations are of the same order.

Both in Table 3 of this study and in *RF/Sounds*, Table 17, the extraordinary frequency of /i/ is due to its inclusion of the high front unstressed vowel, schwi (*vide supra*, Ch. 2, pp. 14–15), with the normal /i/. Were these two separated, as in Appendix C and *RF/Sounds*, Table 15, each would appear in the frequency order immediately adjacent to schwa.

Table 4, abridged from *RF/Sounds*, Appendix D, which gives the relative frequency of occurrence of the *letters* of the Roman alphabet, is presented primarily to emphasize the conspicuous *lack* of relationship between the letters and the phonemes of English spelling. It is this lack which invalidates much of the reasoning back of many efforts at employing "phonics" as an aid to reading and/or spelling.

A similar source of error is that most reading (or writing) methods which take account of spelling frequencies at all concern themselves chiefly with the spellings of sounds (Table 5). It is their disregard of the converse aspect, pronunciations of spellings (Table 6), which most often impairs their effectiveness or invalidates the findings of research. Thus, Lee, in his investigation of the effect of spelling irregularities on reading, took as his sole standard of regularity the statement: "A 'regularly spelt word' can only mean a spoken word, each of whose phonemes is spelt as that

Table 3 Relative frequency of English phonemes

On the 41 phonemes-plus-*the* basis of the SSA phonemic alphabet
Arranged in order of frequency of occurrences

Phoneme	%	Occurrences	Items	Spellings	Phoneme	%	Occurrences	Items	Spellings
i	8.04	29,283	5,962	20	f	1.89	6,889	1,131	7
n	7.40	26,982	4,411	9	h	1.86	6,759	484	3
t	7.30	26,609	4,496	9	b	1.84	6,721	1,152	2
r	7.00	25,471	5,424	10	ʋ	1.72	6,273	1,118	10
s	4.68	17,081	4,162	9	o	1.67	6,091	1,188	19
d	4.32	15,723	3,052	4	ɯ	1.66	6,051	322	19
ə	4.12	15,024	3,273	23	ȧ	1.64	5,961	859	14
l	3.82	13,940	3,274	7	ħ	1.49	5,447	113	1
a	3.80	13,852	1,565	4	ɔ	1.27	4,691	442	13
e	3.50	12,709	3,172	10	ŋ	.98	3,550	1,035	3
z	3.04	11,089	2,063	7	ʃ	.84	3,045	850	15
ɒ	2.89	10,521	1,103	7	g	.77	2,794	636	4
m	2.82	10,281	1,820	5	u	.71	2,577	466	11
k	2.75	10,010	2,680	11	ɑu	.64	2,312	256	5
v	2.31	8,417	905	4	y	.62	2,260	250	6
ɑ	2.15	7,770	1,446	19	ꞓ	.53	1,931	348	5
w	2.12	7,741	553	5	ɑ	.50	1,831	332	9
p	2.09	7,638	1,967	2	j	.44	1,582	492	10
ƀ	2.00	7,310	1	1	ɦ	.38	1,396	213	2
ɛ	1.95	7,114	834	20	ɯ̇	.31	1,138	322	10
					ɔi	.09	347	105	3
					ʒ	.05	170	52	5
					24 consonants	61.34	223,526	41,563	145
					17 vowels	36.66	133,545	22,765	216
					ƀ	2.00	7,310	1	1
					TOTALS 42	100.00	364,381	64,329	362

phoneme is most often spelt in the language";[1] ignoring the aspect of the most frequent pronunciations of the graphemes thus selected. The result of this half-portion definition was that, by his criteria, 72 different pronunciations of the nonsense word *asefo* would be rated as *completely* regular, and

[1] W. R. Lee, *Spelling irregularity and reading difficulty in English* (London: The National Foundation for Educational Research in England and Wales, 1960), p. 26.

Table 4 Relative frequency of letters in English

Arranged in order of frequency

Letter	Percent	Occur-rences	Items
e	12.68	55,465	9,493
t	9.78	42,815	5,366
a	7.88	34,536	5,352
o	7.76	33,993	4,305
i	7.07	30,955	6,058
n	7.06	30,902	5,480
s	6.31	27,642	6,069
r	5.94	26,051	5,569
h	5.73	25,138	1,634
l	3.94	17,261	3,668
d	3.89	17,046	3,394
u	2.89	12,285	2,448
c	2.68	11,747	3,148
f	2.56	11,199	1,164
m	2.44	10,678	1,916
w	2.14	9,396	712
y	2.02	8,837	1,189
g	1.87	8,191	2,079
p	1.86	8,162	2,154
b	1.56	6,838	1,207
v	1.02	4,481	907
k	.60	2,610	526
x	.16	687	214
j	.10	421	117
q	.09	403	122
z	.06	284	131
TOTALS	100.00	438,023	74,422

152 more pronunciations would be rated in his A group as relatively regular!

In studying Table 5 which follows, the ratios, especially of graphemes to phonemes, shown in the summary, will be found instructive.

Tables 7 and 8, in the next chapter, are also pertinent here, but as their data, like those of Table 6, Pronunciations of spellings, are broken down by form of grapheme, they are more appropriately considered there.

Table 5 Relative frequency of spellings of sounds

On the 41-phonemes-plus-*the* basis of the SSA phonemic alphabet
Phonemes are arranged in the order of the phonemic alphabet, Table 1
Under each phoneme, graphemes are arranged in order of frequency of occurrence

How to read this table:
In the material examined, the phoneme /p/ is represented by 2 different graphemes. The phoneme occurs 7,638 times in 1,967 different items (syllables or words). Of these, the grapheme *p* represents 7,276 occurrences in 1,850 different items; of which 5,211 occurrences in 1,290 different items are the first phoneme of the syllable, 813 occurrences in 265 different items are medial (neither the first nor last phoneme of the syllable), and 1,252 occurrences in 295 different items are the last phoneme of the syllable.

Phoneme	Grapheme	Phoneme totals		Grapheme totals		Initial		Medial		Final		Syllabic	
		Oc	It	Oc	It	Oc	It	Oc	It	Oc	It	Oc	It
/p/		7,638	1,967										
2	p			7,276	1,850	5,211	1,290	813	265	1,252	295		
	pp			362	117	188	63	21	8	153	46		
/b/		6,721	1,152										
2	b			6,686	1,130	6,050	925	44	21	592	184		
	bb			35	22			4	3	31	19		
/t/		26,609	4,496										
9	t			24,998	4,122	9,529	1,695	2,404	654	13,065	1,773		
	tt			751	152	122	28	2	1	627	123		

—/**t**/	ed			442	140					442	140
	d			220	65					220	65
	tw			146	1	146	1				
	bt			40	11			3	2	37	9
	pt			9	2			1	1	8	1
	ct			2	2					2	2
	cht			1	1					1	1
/**d**/		15,723	3,052								
4	d			14,285	2,723	4,265	1,072	516	144	9,504	1,507
	ed			767	282					767	282
	ld			533	6					533	6
	dd			138	41	45	7	6	2	87	32
/**k**/		10,010	2,680								
11	c			6,403	1,775	4,323	1,126	722	210	1,358	439
	k			1,854	343	272	72	300	82	1,282	189
	½x			510	165			507	164	3	1
	ck			452	151			88	43	364	108
	q			377	110	333	87	28	11	16	12
	cc			144	45	113	35			41	10
	ch			122	47	60	27	49	12	13	8
	x			68	17					68	17
	lk			52	12			19	6	33	6
	cq			15	10	11	7			4	3
	½xi			13	5	1	1			12	4

Pho-neme	Graph-eme	Phoneme totals Oc	Phoneme totals It	Grapheme totals Oc	Grapheme totals It	Initial Oc	Initial It	Medial Oc	Medial It	Final Oc	Final It	Syllabic Oc	Syllabic It
/g/		2,794	636										
4	g			2,616	560	2,248	437	24	12	344	111		
	½x			104	31			103	30	1	1		
	gg			70	42	6	3	16	8	48	31		
	gh			4	3	4	3						
/f/		6,889	1,131										
7	f			6,117	954	5,104	818	115	37	898	99		
	ff			510	102	178	39	9	8	323	55		
	ph			108	60	80	42	6	5	22	13		
	lf			63	2					63	2		
	gh			59	8					59	8		
	ft			31	4					31	4		
	pph			1	1					1	1		
/v/		8,417	905										
4	v			4,403	899	1,630	447	341	86	2,432	366		
	f			4,001	3					4,001	3		
	ve			12	2					12	2		
	lv			1	1			1	1				

/ħ/		1,396	213											
2	th			1,392	212									
	h			4	1					4	1			
/ħ/		5,447	113											
1	th			5,447	113	4,106	48	14	7	1,327	58			
/s/		17,081	4,162											
9	s			12,822	2,974	6,663	1,485	1,846	352	4,313	1,137			
	c			2,477	622	980	279	130	34	1,367	309			
	ss			1,156	342	118	45	79	26	959	271			
	½x			495	162			71	10	424	152			
	sc			55	33	35	19			20	14			
	st			35	17			1	1	34	16			
	sw			34	6	34	6							
	z			5	4	1	1			4	3			
	ps			2	2	2	2							
/z/		11,089	2,063											
7	s			10,695	1,902	432	119	181	40	10,074	1,740		8	3
	z			247	107	81	26	68	29	98	52			
	½x			103	30					103	30			
	ss			25	11	24	10			1	1			
	zz			10	7					10	7			
	sc			8	5	7	4			1	1			
	x			1	1	1	1							

Phoneme	Grapheme	Phoneme totals Oc	Phoneme totals It	Grapheme totals Oc	Grapheme totals It	Initial Oc	Initial It	Medial Oc	Medial It	Final Oc	Final It	Syllabic Oc	Syllabic It
/ʃ/		3,045	850										
15	ti			1,360	418	1,157	379			203	39		
	sh			1,178	278	853	151	78	24	245	102	2	1
	ci			182	47	39	13			143	34		
	ssi			77	28					77	28		
	ss			65	14	15	7			50	7		
	s			58	10	58	10						
	ch			38	11	36	9			2	2		
	si			22	15	22	15						
	c			17	11	17	11						
	sci			17	5	15	4			2	1		
	½xi			12	4	12	4						
	ce			7	1	7	1						
	t			7	6	4	3			3	3		
	½x			3	1	3	1						
	sc			2	1	2	1						
/ʒ/		170	52										
5	si			81	24	34	14			47	10		
	s			78	20	30	7			48	13		
	g			6	5			2	1	4	4		
	z			4	2	4	2						
	½x			1	1	1	1						

/c/		1,931	348										
5	ch			1,457	215	447	124	50	16	960	75		
	t			329	85	258	72			71	13		
	tch			85	36			12	4	73	32		
	ti			56	10	56	10						
	te			4	2	4	2						
/j/		1,582	492										
10	g			948	306	299	113	70	18	579	175		
	j			414	111	411	109			3	2		
	dg			95	35			9	7	86	28		
	di			42	6	42	6						
	d			38	16	4	3			34	13		
	gi			30	7	19	4			11	3		
	dj			7	6	7	6						
	ge			4	2	4	2						
	de			2	2	2	2						
	gg			2	1					2	1		
/m/		10,218	1,820										
5	m			10,049	1,727	5,698	926	554	155	3,757	626	40	20
	mm			182	70	110	34	1	1	71	35		
	mn			20	9			10	4	10	5		
	lm			17	5					17	5		
	mb			13	9			5	3	8	6		

Pho-neme	Graph-eme	Phoneme totals Oc	Phoneme totals It	Grapheme totals Oc	Grapheme totals It	Initial Oc	Initial It	Medial Oc	Medial It	Final Oc	Final It	Syllabic Oc	Syllabic It
/n/		26,982	4,411										
9	n			25,727	4,168	3,539	625	8,453	1,212	13,720	2,323	15	8
	en			570	116	62	27	27	7	184	19	297	63
	kn			259	21	259	21						
	nn			249	54	61	19	5	2	183	33		
	on			105	29	7	5	19	4	47	13	32	7
	gn			66	19			21	8	45	11		
	pn			3	1	3	1						
	nd			2	2					2	2		
	in			1	1							1	1
/ŋ/		3,550	1,035										
3	ng			3,164	911			202	56	2,962	855		
	n			385	123			294	70	91	53		
	nd			1	1					1	1		
/l/		13,940	3,274										
7	l			10,288	2,621	4,214	990	3,110	882	2,962	747	2	2
	ll			2,519	342	148	56	174	50	2,195	23	2	2
	le			1,106	301	52	29	112	51	684	180	258	41
	il			20	5	5	2	2	1	8	1	5	1

—/**l**/	sl			5	3	3	2			2	1
	al			1	1					1	1
	ual			1	1	1	1				
/**r**/		25,471	5,424								
10	r			24,911	5,237	3,412	1,015	9,271	2,406	12,228	1,816
	rr			400	143	99	36	31	11	270	96
	wr			122	22	122	22				
	½re			13	10			6	4	7	6
	re			8	1					8	1
	l			5	3					5	3
	rh			5	5	5	5				
	rps			5	1					5	1
	rrh			1	1	1	1				
	rt			1	1					1	1
/**w**/		7,741	553								
5	w			5,527	380	5,335	330	192	50		
	½wh			1,359	48			1,359	48		
	½o-e			450	5	450	5				
	u			404	119	11	9	393	110		
	½oi			1	1			1	1		

Phoneme	Grapheme	Phoneme totals Oc	Phoneme totals It	Grapheme totals Oc	Grapheme totals It	Initial Oc	Initial It	Medial Oc	Medial It	Final Oc	Final It	Syllabic Oc	Syllabic It
/y/		2,260	250										
6	y			1,507	40	1,507	40						
	½u			357	148	357	148						
	½u-e			182	18	182	18						
	i			145	36	144	35	1	1				
	½ue			68	7	68	7						
	½ew			1	1	1	1						
/h/		6,759	484										
3	h			5,023	427	5,023	427						
	½wh			1,359	48	1,359	48						
	wh			377	9	377	9						
Consonant phoneme subtotals													
24	145	223,526	41,563										

Pho-neme	Graph-eme	Phoneme totals		Grapheme totals		Initial		Medial		Final		Syllabic	
		Oc	It	Oc	It	Oc	It	Oc	It	Oc	It	Oc	It
/**a**/		13,852	1,565										
4	a			13,174	1,536	6,082	289	6,397	1,031	16	6	679	210
	a-e			665	23	3	2	662	21				
	ua			7	3			7	3				
	au			6	3	1	1	5	2				
/**ɑ**/		1,831	332										
9	a			1,089	280	178	47	851	209	59	23	1	1
	a-e			661	22	549	2	112	20				
	ea			31	11			31	11				
	au			17	6			17	6				
	ua			15	8			15	8				
	ah			10	1							10	1
	e			4	2	1	1	3	1				
	aa			3	1			3	1				
	½oi			1	1					1	1		
/**e**/		12,709	3,172										
10	e			10,987	2,941	3,315	1,159	7,538	1,749	41	15	93	18
	e-e			530	96	314	36	216	60				
	ea			402	105			402	105				
	a			371	10	261	7	104	1	6	2		
	ai			298	4			298	4				
	ay			52	1			52	1				

Pho-neme	Graph-eme	Phoneme totals Oc	Phoneme totals It	Grapheme totals Oc	Grapheme totals It	Initial Oc	Initial It	Medial Oc	Medial It	Final Oc	Final It	Syllabic Oc	Syllabic It
—/e/	ie			40	5			40	5				
	ue			21	5			21	5				
	e-ue			7	4	3	1	4	3				
	u			1	1			1	1				
/ɑ/		7,770	1,446										
19	a			2,149	650	75	41	500	183	1,123	355	451	71
	a-e			1,918	355	46	19	1,870	334	2	2		
	ay			1,109	90			197	25	912	65		
	ai			906	244	82	17	815	221	9	6		
	ey			508	12			20	5	488	7		
	e-e			464	24	1	1	463	23				
	ei			323	6			323	6				
	ea			244	20			244	20				
	eigh			82	19	10	4	47	7	25	8		
	ai-e			29	11	6	3	23	8				
	aigh			22	5			22	5				
	e			7	3			6	2	1	1		
	a-ue			2	1			2	1				
	ue			2	1			2	1				
	au-e			1	1			1	1				
	aye			1	1			1	1				

—/**ɑ**/	é			1	1					1	1		
	ee			1	1					1	1		
	eh			1	1							1	1
/**i**/		29,283	5,962										
20	i			20,276	3,807	9,546	1,482	8,348	1,422	939	450	1,443	453
	y			4,100	885			114	50	2,705	630	1,281	205
	e			2,833	803	62	7	37	8	2,362	644	372	144
	i-e			537	151	58	22	479	129				
	ee			367	6			331	3	1	1	35	2
	ie			338	121	83	19	252	100	3	2		
	a-e			296	94	169	53	127	41				
	u			104	4			104	4				
	ey			102	22	3	2	5	5	30	10	64	5
	ui			87	16	1	1	86	15				
	ai			77	15			75	13	1	1	1	1
	o			48	2			48	2				
	u-e			30	3	30	3						
	a			29	15	16	9	13	6				
	ei			22	3	21	2	1	1				
	hi			12	5	3	3					9	2
	e-e			10	4	3	1	7	3				
	ia			7	3	6	2			1	1		
	ia-e			7	2	7	2						
	oi			1	1							1	1

Pho-neme	Graph-eme	Phoneme totals		Grapheme totals		Initial		Medial		Final		Syllabic	
		Oc	It	Oc	It	Oc	It	Oc	It	Oc	It	Oc	It
/ɛ/		7,114	834										
20	e			3,333	205	95	2	51	27	3,142	164	45	12
	ea			1,385	266	153	18	1,068	210	155	35	9	3
	ee			1,158	175	12	5	860	141	284	27	2	2
	e-e			444	46	27	5	417	41				
	eo			180	3					180	3		
	ea-e			175	27	10	3	165	24				
	ie			111	36			111	36				
	ie-e			87	14			87	14				
	ei			72	13			13	6	23	6	36	1
	ei-e			64	11			64	11				
	i-e			63	14	1	1	62	13				
	i			16	8			13	5	3	3		
	ee-e			10	6			10	6				
	ea-ue			5	1			5	1				
	i-ue			4	3			4	3				
	ey			3	2			1	1	2	1		
	ae			1	1					1	1		
	e'e			1	1	1	1						
	oe			1	1					1	1		
	ui			1	1					1	1		

/ɒ/		10,521	1,103										
7	o			9,150	1,022	5,190	116	3,652	817	189	59	119	30
	a			1,215	35			1,215	35				
	au			42	9	3	2					39	7
	o-e			35	21			35	21				
	ho			34	6	34	6						
	ow			32	5			32	5				
	o-ue			13	5			13	5				
/ɔ/		4,691	442										
13	o			2,595	219	693	35	1,902	184				
	a			1,424	107	706	18	663	81	55	8		
	aw			184	34			45	11	115	21	24	2
	au-e			161	7			161	7				
	ough			152	9			152	9				
	au			69	38	2	2	22	12	6	5	39	19
	o-e			43	10			43	10				
	augh			32	8			27	6	5	2		
	oa			15	3			15	3				
	a-e			9	4			9	4				
	ao			3	1			3	1				
	hau			3	1	3	1						
	awe			1	1							1	1

Pho-neme	Graph-eme	Phoneme totals Oc	Phoneme totals It	Grapheme totals Oc	Grapheme totals It	Initial Oc	Initial It	Medial Oc	Medial It	Final Oc	Final It	Syllabic Oc	Syllabic It
/ʊ/		6,273	1,118										
10	u			3,768	797	1,076	227	2,591	545	101	25		
	o			857	104	261	6	596	98				
	o-e			565	34			565	34				
	ou			527	157	135	70	391	86	1	1		
	½o-e			450	5			450	5				
	oe			63	2			63	2				
	u-e			19	9			19	9				
	oo			17	7			17	7				
	o-ue			6	2			6	2				
	u-ue			1	1			1	1				
/o/		6,091	1,188										
19	o			3,584	755	308	8	883	190	1,879	400	514	157
	o-e			1,199	183	3	2	1,193	180	3	1		
	ow			671	106	132	18	121	25	326	41	92	22
	oa			243	72	13	6	229	65				
	ou			117	21			117	21				
	ough			65	7					60	5	5	2
	ou-e			56	4			56	4				
	oh			53	1							53	1

—/**o**/	oe			38	13	1	1	32	9	5	3		
	oo			27	6			27	6				
	au			7	4			1	1	6	3		
	ew			7	5			4	2	3	3		
	oa-e			7	4			7	4				
	eau			6	1					6	1		
	ot			6	2			5	1	1	1		
	owe			2	1							2	1
	au-e			1	1			1	1				
	eo			1	1					1	1		
	o-ue			1	1			1	1				
/**u**/		2,577	466										
11	u			604	171	7	4	377	101	111	39	109	27
	ou			546	8			546	8				
	oo			388	54			388	54				
	o			368	14			1	1	367	13		
	u-e			297	78	56	12	241	66				
	½u			257	117			12	5	245	112		
	½u-e			57	9			57	9				
	ue			40	9	19	4	2	2	2	1	17	2
	½ue			18	4			16	3	2	1		
	½ew			1	1					1	1		
	ugh			1	1							1	1

Phoneme	Grapheme	Phoneme totals Oc	Phoneme totals It	Grapheme totals Oc	Grapheme totals It	Initial Oc	Initial It	Medial Oc	Medial It	Final Oc	Final It	Syllabic Oc	Syllabic It
/ɯ/		6,051	322										
19	o			3,645	26			59	13	3,586	13		
	ou			1,127	36			339	26	788	10		
	oo			430	88	1	1	370	84	59	3		
	u			161	48			77	19	84	29		
	½u-e			125	9			97	8	28	1		
	o-e			112	15			112	15				
	½u			100	30			39	9	61	21		
	ough			92	2					92	2		
	u-e			79	19			79	19				
	½ue			51	4			5	2	46	2		
	ue			44	5			2	2	42	3		
	ou-e			23	4			23	4				
	ew			22	12			4	4	18	8		
	ui			15	10			15	10				
	oe			11	5			4	2	7	3		
	oo-e			11	6	1	1	10	5				
	eu			1	1					1	1		
	oeu			1	1					1	1		
	ui-e			1	1			1	1				

/ə/		15,024	3,273										
23	a			5,602	1,105	845	229	1,117	334	471	213	3,169	329
	e			5,027	1,051	2,465	567	2,518	471	24	9	20	4
	o			2,901	787	650	172	2,245	611	3	3	3	1
	u			369	107	8	4	361	103				
	e-e			360	27			360	27				
	i			330	57	1	1	328	55			1	1
	a-e			148	51	47	22	101	29				
	ea			143	30	64	11	79	19				
	o-e			60	5	1	1	59	4				
	ou			22	11	1	1	21	10				
	u-e			17	10	5	2	12	8				
	½re			13	10			13	10				
	½i-o			8	3	8	3						
	eu			6	6			6	6				
	o-o			5	3			5	3				
	eo			3	1	3	1						
	io			3	2	3	2						
	ue			2	2	1	1	1	1				
	ea-e			1	1			1	1				
	ha			1	1	1	1						
	oi			1	1	1	1						
	uo			1	1	1	1						
	y			1	1			1	1				

Pho-neme	Graph-eme	Phoneme totals Oc	Phoneme totals It	Grapheme totals Oc	Grapheme totals It	Initial Oc	Initial It	Medial Oc	Medial It	Final Oc	Final It	Syllabic Oc	Syllabic It
/ie/		5,961	859										
14	i			2,107	302	71	11	529	149	274	120	1,233	22
	i-e			1,802	324	78	25	1,724	299				
	y			1,154	73			3	3	1,151	70		
	igh			546	74			447	63	99	11		
	ie			153	49			139	43	14	6		
	eigh			57	4	33	1	6	2			18	1
	eye			55	4	36	2					19	2
	uy			37	6			2	2	35	4		
	y-e			31	11			31	11				
	½i-o			8	3							8	3
	ui-e			6	5			6	5				
	ai-e			2	1	2	1						
	ye			2	2			1	1	1	1		
	ui			1	1			1	1				
/oi/		347	105										
3	oi			165	66	21	2	135	56	9	8		
	oy			152	32			51	6	101	26		
	oi-e			30	7			30	7				

/au/		2,312	256								
5	ou			1,422	150	690	34	678	111	54	5
	ow			632	56			169	28	463	28
	ou-e			194	40	1	1	96	19	97	20
	hou			55	4	55	4				
	ough			9	6			7	4	2	2
/iu/		1,138	322								
10	u			498	186			138	39	360	147
	u-e			248	81			248	81		
	ew			229	19			30	4	199	15
	ue			53	14			8	4	45	10
	iew			43	8			9	4	34	4
	eau			24	3					24	3
	ui			22	5			22	5		
	eu			18	3					18	3
	ieu			2	2					2	2
	eu-e			1	1			1	1		
Vowel phoneme subtotals											
17	216	133,545	22,765								

Summary

Phonemes	Graphemes	Phoneme totals Oc	Phoneme totals It	Graphemes / Phonemes	:	Ratio	Occurrences / Items	:	Ratio
Consonants									
24	145	223,526	41,563	145 / 24		6.0	223,526 / 41,563		5.4
Vowels									
17	216	133,545	22,765	216 / 17		12.7	133,545 / 22,765		5.9
Subtotals									
41	361	357,071	64,328	361 / 41		8.8	357,071 / 64,328		5.6
Wordsign /ðə/									
1	1	7,310	1						
TOTALS									
42	362	364,381	64,329	362 / 42		8.6	364,381 / 64,329		5.7

Chapter 5

Pronunciations of spellings (Grapheme-phoneme correspondences)

The data of Table 6, Pronunciations of spellings, like the corresponding data of *Hws*, are broken down into three groups according to the forms of the graphemes: single letters, simple digraphs, and all other spellings. Both in the main table and its summary, and in the two following supplementary tables, this separation helps to give a clearer view of the vagaries of our traditional orthography, and one more readily appraised in quantitative terms. Thus in the summary, note that over 80% of all occurrences of phonemes are represented by single-letter graphemes, thereby throwing on the single letters a particularly heavy burden of multiple meanings, an average of 3.0 meanings per letter; for the 5 vowel letters, 35 meanings, an average of 7.0 meanings per letter.

Table 7, Distribution of spellings by frequency of occurrence (more fully discussed in Chapter 6), throws an important light on the weight to be attached to the frequency of a particular spelling, whether in terms of priority of emphasis in employing existing teaching materials, or in its use or avoidance at a particular stage in creating new teaching materials.

Table 8, Comparative dispersion of spellings, offers one more sidelight on relative importance. Horn,[1] in his list of

[1] Ernest Horn, *A basic writing vocabulary: 10,000 words most commonly used in writing* (Iowa City, Iowa: College of Education, University of Iowa, 1926), pp. 26, 47.

10,000 words most commonly used in writing, laid so much stress on the appearance of a word in more than one category of the material examined (chiefly business correspondence) that he weighted his raw data by a factor of from 1 to 5 to reflect this diversity, thereby greatly impairing the value of the reported results as a basis for phonemic analysis.[2] The material of *RF/Sounds* was so well diversified in the first place that any such treatment of those data seemed quite unnecessary, but the comparisons in Table 7 are, I believe, significant. Note particularly three points:

1. This study finds in 100,000 running words almost ⅔ of the different spellings identified in the dictionary.

2. This study finds, in 10,119 different words found in 100,000 running words, about 10% more spellings than Hanna found in 17,310 different words from at least 4½ million running words. This reflects chiefly, I believe, the more careful diversification of my material[3] as compared with the Thorndike-Lorge list used by Hanna.

3. The 270 spellings common to both studies include 218 of the 255 spellings reported in Table 6 as occurring oftener than 10 times. This clearly suggests that frequencies within that range are of practical significance.

This chapter completes, except for the appendixes already noted, the reported data of this study, which, to keep the bulk of its findings within measurable bounds, has confined itself to the graphemes corresponding to single phonemes. However, my earlier study of phonemes, *RF/Sounds*, included in its published report not only an exhaustive analysis of the relative frequency of single phonemes but also detailed studies, arranged by initial phoneme, by final phoneme, and by vowel, of the 1,397 syllables (out of a total of about 4,400) which made up over 93% of the material investigated; together with tables of the "1,000 commonest" words which may be expected to make up at least 75% of any normal connected matter. In consequence, anyone with a fairly broad linguistic background, seeking to go beyond the findings here reported, should be able to

[2] See *RF/Sounds* (1950), Addenda, p. 186.

[3] For complete list of sources, see *RF/Sounds*, Table 1, pp. 8–9.

extract from the phonemic study a substantial amount of additional graphemic information. Just this was, in fact, done in connection with some of the most important previous efforts to develop an efficient phonemic notation for English, including the Anglic of Zachrisson,[4] the New Spelling of the British Simplified Spelling Society,[5] and more recently, Sir James Pitman's i.t.a.[6]

[4] R. E. Zachrisson, *Anglic*, 2nd enlarged ed. (Cambridge, England: W. Heffer & Sons, Ltd., 1932).

[5] Ripman, *et al.*, *New Spelling*, 6th ed. (1948).

[6] Pitman, *Alphabets and reading* (1969).

Table 6 Relative frequency of pronunciations of spellings

On the 41-phoneme-plus-*the* basis of the SSA phonemic alphabet
Graphemes arranged in 3 groups: single letters, simple digraphs, all other spellings
In each group, graphemes are arranged alphabetically
Under each grapheme, phonemes are arranged in order of frequency of occurrence

How to read this table:

In the material examined, the grapheme *a* represents 8 different phonemes. The grapheme occurs 25,053 times in 3,738 different items (syllables or words). Of these, the grapheme *a* represents the phoneme /a/ in 13,174 occurences in 1,536 different items; of which 6,082 occurrences in 289 different items are the first phoneme of the syllable, 6,397 occurrences in 1,031 different items are medial (neither the first nor last phoneme of the syllable), 16 occurrences in 6 different items are the last phoneme of the syllable, and 679 occurrences in 210 different items are syllabic (the only phoneme in the syllable).

Single letters

Grapheme	Phoneme	Grapheme totals		Phoneme totals		Initial		Medial		Final		Syllabic	
		Oc	It	Oc	It	Oc	It	Oc	It	Oc	It	Oc	It
a		25,053	3,738										
8	/a/			13,174	1,536	6,082	289	6,397	1,031	16	6	679	210
	/ə/			5,602	1,105	845	229	1,117	334	471	213	3,169	329
	/ɑ/			2,149	650	75	41	500	183	1,123	355	451	71
	/ɔ/			1,424	107	706	18	663	81	55	8		
	/ɒ/			1,215	35			1,215	35				
	/α/			1,089	280	178	47	851	209	59	23	1	1
	/e/			371	10	261	7	104	1	6	2		
	/i/			29	15	16	9	13	6				

b		6,686	1,130										
1	/b/			6,686	1,130	6,050	925	44	21	592	184		
c		8,897	2,408										
3	/k/			6,403	1,775	4,323	1,126	722	210	1,359	439		
	/s/			2,477	622	980	279	130	34	1,367	309		
	/ʃ/			17	11	17	11						
d		14,543	2,804										
3	/d/			14,285	2,723	4,265	1,072	516	144	9,504	1,507		
	/t/			220	65					220	65		
	/j/			38	16	4	3			34	13		
e		22,191	5,005										
6	/e/			10,987	2,941	3,315	1,159	7,538	1,749	41	15	93	18
	/ə/			5,027	1,051	2,465	567	2,518	471	24	9	20	4
	/ɛ/			3,333	205	95	2	51	27	3,142	164		
	/i/			2,833	803	62	7	37	8	2,362	644	372	144
	/ɑ/			7	3			6	2	1	1		
	/ɑ/			4	2	1	1	3	1				
f		10,118	957										
2	/f/			6,117	954	5,104	818	115	37	898	99		
	/v/			4,001	3					4,001	3		

Grapheme	Phoneme	Grapheme totals Oc	Grapheme totals It	Phoneme totals Oc	Phoneme totals It	Initial Oc	Initial It	Medial Oc	Medial It	Final Oc	Final It	Syllabic Oc	Syllabic It
g		3,570	871										
3	/g/			2,616	560	2,248	437	24	12	344	111		
	/j/			948	306	299	113	70	18	579	175		
	/ʒ/			6	5			2	1	4	4		
h		5,027	428										
2	/h/			5,023	427	5,023	427						
	/ћ/			4	1					4	1		
i		22,874	4,210										
5	/i/			20,276	3,807	9,546	1,482	8,348	1,422	939	450	1,443	453
	/ȧ/			2,107	302	71	11	529	149	274	120	1,233	22
	/ə/			330	57	1	1	328	55			1	1
	/y/			145	36	144	35	1	1				
	/ɛ/			16	8			13	5	3	3		
j		414	111										
1	/j/			414	111	411	109			3	2		
k		1,854	343										
1	/k/			1,854	343	272	72	300	82	1,282	189		

l		10,293	2,624										
2	/l/			10,288	2,621	4,214	990	3,110	882	2,962	747	2	2
	/r/			5	3					5	3		
m		10,049	1,727										
1	/m/			10,049	1,727	5,699	927	554	155	3,757	626	39	19
n		26,112	4,291										
2	/n/			25,727	4,168	3,539	625	8,453	1,212	13,720	2,323	15	8
	/ŋ/			385	123			294	70	91	53		
o		23,148	2,929										
8	/ɒ/			9,150	1,022	5,190	116	3,652	817	189	59	119	30
	/ɯ/			3,645	26			59	13	3,586	13		
	/o/			3,584	755	308	8	883	190	1,879	400	514	157
	/ə/			2,901	787	650	172	2,245	611	3	3	3	1
	/ɔ/			2,595	219	693	35	1,902	184				
	/ʊ/			857	104	261	6	596	98				
	/u/			368	14			1	1	367	13		
	/i/			48	2			48	2				
p		7,276	1,850										
1	/p/			7,276	1,850	5,211	1,290	813	265	1,252	295		
q		377	110										
1	/k/			377	110	333	87	28	11	16	12		

Grapheme	Phoneme	Grapheme totals Oc	Grapheme totals It	Phoneme totals Oc	Phoneme totals It	Initial Oc	Initial It	Medial Oc	Medial It	Final Oc	Final It	Syllabic Oc	Syllabic It
r		24,911	5,237										
1	/r/			24,911	5,237	3,412	1,015	9,271	2,406	12,228	1,816		
s		23,653	4,906										
4	/s/			12,822	2,974	6,663	1,485	1,846	352	4,313	1,137		
	/z/			10,695	1,902	432	119	181	40	10,074	1,740	8	3
	/ʒ/			78	20	30	7			48	13		
	/ʃ/			58	10	58	10						
t		25,334	4,213										
3	/t/			24,998	4,122								
	/č/			329	85	258	72			71	13		
	/ʃ/			7	6	4	3			3	3		
u		5,909	1,433										
8	/ʊ/			3,768	797	1,076	227	2,591	545	101	25		
	/u/			604	171	7	4	377	101	111	39	109	27
	/iɯ/			498	186			138	39	360	147		
	/w/			404	119	11	9	393	110				
	/ə/			369	107	8	4	361	103				
	/ɯ/			161	48			77	19	84	29		
	/i/			104	4			104	4				
	/e/			1	1			1	1				

v		4,403	899								
1	/v/			4,403	899	1,630	447	341	86	2,432	366
w		5,527	380								
1	/w/			5,527	380	5,335	330	192	50		
x		69	18								
2	/k/			68	17					68	17
	/z/			1	1	1	1				
y		6,762	999								
4	/i/			4,100	885			114	50	2,705	630
	/y/			1,507	40	1,507	40				
	/ȧ/			1,154	73			3	3	1,151	70
	/ə/			1	1			1	1		
z		256	113								
3	/z/			247	107	81	26	68	29	98	52
	/s/			5	4	1	1			4	3
	/ʒ/			4	2	4	2				
Single letter totals											
26	77	295,306	53,734								

Grapheme	Phoneme	Grapheme totals Oc	Grapheme totals It	Phoneme totals Oc	Phoneme totals It	Initial Oc	Initial It	Medial Oc	Medial It	Final Oc	Final It	Syllabic Oc	Syllabic It
Simple digraphs													
aa		3	1										
1	/ɑ/			3	1			3	1				
ae		1	1										
1	/ɛ/			1	1					1	1		
ah		10	1										
1	/ɑ/			10	1							10	1
ai		1,281	263										
3	/ɑ/			906	244	82	17	815	221	9	6		
	/e/			298	4			298	4				
	/i/			77	15			75	13	1	1	1	1
al		1	1										
1	/l/			1	1					1	1		
ao		3	1										
1	/ɔ/			3	1			3	1				

au		141	60										
5	/ɔ/			69	38	2	2	22	12	6	5	39	19
	/ɒ/			42	9	3	2					39	7
	/ɑ/			17	6			17	6				
	/o/			7	4			1	1	6	3		
	/a/			6	3	1	1	5	2				
aw		184	34										
1	/ɔ/			184	34			45	11	115	21	24	2
ay		1,161	91										
2	/ɑ/			1,109	90			197	25	912	65		
	/e/			52	1			52	1				
bb		35	22										
1	/b/			35	22			4	3	31	19		
bt		40	11										
1	/t/			40	11			3	2	37	9		
cc		144	45										
1	/k/			144	45	113	35			41	10		
ce		7	1										
1	/ʃ/			7	1	7	1						

Grapheme	Phoneme	Grapheme totals Oc	Grapheme totals It	Phoneme totals Oc	Phoneme totals It	Initial Oc	Initial It	Medial Oc	Medial It	Final Oc	Final It	Syllabic Oc	Syllabic It
ch		1,617	273										
3	/č/			1,457	215	447	124	50	16	960	75		
	/k/			122	47	60	27	49	12	13	8		
	/ʃ/			38	11	36	9			2	2		
ci		182	47										
1	/ʃ/			182	47	39	13			143	34		
ck		452	151										
1	/k/			452	151			88	43	364	108		
cq		15	10										
1	/k/			15	10	11	7			4	3		
ct		2	2										
1	/t/			2	2					2	2		
dd		138	41										
1	/d/			138	41	45	7	6	2	87	32		
de		2	2										
1	/j/			2	2	2	2						

dg		95	35										
1	/j/			95	35			9	7	86	28		
di		42	6										
1	/j/			42	6	42	6						
dj		7	6										
1	/j/			7	6	7	6						
ea		2,205	432										
5	/ɛ/			1,385	266	153	18	1,068	210	155	35	9	3
	/e/			402	105			402	105				
	/ɑ/			244	20			244	20				
	/ə/			143	30	64	11	79	19				
	/ɑ/			31	11			31	11				
ed		1,209	422										
2	/d/			767	282					767	282		
	/t/			442	140					442	140		
ee		1,526	182										
3	/ɛ/			1,158	175	12	5	860	141	284	27	2	2
	/i/			367	6			331	3	1	1	35	2
	/ɑ/			1	1					1	1		
eh		1	1										
1	/ɑ/			1	1							1	1

Grapheme	Phoneme	Grapheme totals Oc	Grapheme totals It	Phoneme totals Oc	Phoneme totals It	Initial Oc	Initial It	Medial Oc	Medial It	Final Oc	Final It	Syllabic Oc	Syllabic It
ei		417	22										
3	/ɑ/			323	6			323	6				
	/ɛ/			72	13			13	6	23	6	36	1
	/i/			22	3	21	2	1	1				
en		570	116										
1	/n/			570	116	62	27	27	7	184	18	297	63
eo		184	5										
3	/ɛ/			180	3					180	3		
	/ə/			3	1	3	1						
	/o/			1	1					1	1		
eu		25	10										
3	/ɯ̇/			18	3					18	3		
	/ə/			6	6			6	6				
	/ɯ/			1	1					1	1		
ew		258	36										
3	/ɯ̇/			229	19			30	4	199	15		
	/ɯ/			22	12			4	4	18	8		
	/o/			7	5			4	2	3	3		

ey		613	36										
3	/ɑ/			508	12			20	5	488	7		
	/i/			102	22	3	2	5	5	30	10	64	5
	/ɛ/			3	2			1	1	2	1		
ff		510	102										
1	/f/			510	102	178	39	9	8	323	55		
ft		31	4										
1	/f/			31	4					31	4		
ge		4	2										
1	/j/			4	2	4	2						
gg		72	43										
2	/g/			70	42	6	3	16	8	48	31		
	/j/			2	1					2	1		
gh		63	11										
2	/f/			59	8					59	8		
	/g/			4	3	4	3						
gi		30	7										
1	/j/			30	7	19	4			11	3		
gn		66	19										
1	/n/			66	19			21	8	45	11		

Grapheme	Phoneme	Grapheme totals Oc	Grapheme totals It	Phoneme totals Oc	Phoneme totals It	Initial Oc	Initial It	Medial Oc	Medial It	Final Oc	Final It	Syllabic Oc	Syllabic It
ha		1	1										
1	/ə/			1	1	1	1						
hi		12	5										
1	/i/			12	5	3	3					9	2
ho		34	6										
1	/ɒ/			34	6	34	6						
ia		7	3										
1	/i/			7	3	6	2			1	1		
ie		642	211										
4	/i/			338	121	83	19	252	100	3	2		
	/ȧ/			153	49			139	43	14	6		
	/ɛ/			111	36			111	36				
	/e/			40	5			40	5				
il		20	5										
1	/l/			20	5	5	2	2	1	8	1	5	1

in		1	1										
1	/n/			1	1							1	1
io		3	2										
1	/ə/			3	2	3	2						
kn		259	21										
1	/n/			259	21	259	21						
ld		533	6										
1	/d/			533	6					533	6		
le		1,106	301										
1	/l/			1,106	301	52	29	112	51	684	180	258	41
lf		63	2										
1	/f/			63	2					63	2		
lk		52	12										
1	/k/			52	12			19	6	33	6		
ll		2,519	342										
1	/l/			2,519	342	148	56	174	50	2,195	234	2	2
lm		17	5										
1	/m/			17	5					17	5		
lv		1	1										
1	/v/			1	1			1	1				

Graph-eme	Pho-neme	Grapheme totals Oc	Grapheme totals It	Phoneme totals Oc	Phoneme totals It	Initial Oc	Initial It	Medial Oc	Medial It	Final Oc	Final It	Syllabic Oc	Syllabic It
mb		13	9										
1	/m/			13	9			5	3	8	6		
mm		182	70										
1	/m/			182	70	110	34	1	1	71	35		
mn		20	9										
1	/m/			20	9			10	4	10	5		
nd		3	3										
2	/n/			2	2					2	2		
	/ŋ/			1	1					1	1		
ng		3,164	911										
1	/ŋ/			3,164	911			202	56	2,962	855		
nn		249	54										
1	/n/			249	54	61	19	5	2	183	33		
oa		258	75										
2	/o/			243	72	13	6	229	65	1	1		
	/ɔ/			15	3			15	3				

oe		113	21										
4	/ʊ/			63	2			63	2				
	/o/			38	13	1	1	32	9	5	3		
	/ɯ/			11	5			4	2	7	3		
	/ɛ/			1	1					1	1		
oh		53	1										
1	/o/			53	1							53	1
oi		167	68										
3	/ɔ̇/			165	66	21	2	135	56	9	8		
	/i/			1	1							1	1
	/ə/			1	1	1	1						
on		105	29										
1	/n/			105	29	7	5	19	4	47	13	32	7
oo		862	155										
4	/ɯ/			430	88	1	1	370	84	59	3		
	/u/			388	54			388	54				
	/o/			27	6			27	6				
	/ʊ/			17	7			17	7				
ot		6	2										
1	/o/			6	2			5	1	1	1		

Grapheme	Phoneme	Grapheme totals Oc	Grapheme totals It	Phoneme totals Oc	Phoneme totals It	Initial Oc	Initial It	Medial Oc	Medial It	Final Oc	Final It	Syllabic Oc	Syllabic It
ou		3,761	383										
6	/ɑɪ/			1,422	150	690	34	678	111	54	5		
	/ɯ/			1,127	36			339	26	788	10		
	/u/			546	8			546	8				
	/ʊ/			527	157	135	70	391	86	1	1		
	/o/			117	21			117	21				
	/ə/			22	11	1	1	21	10				
ow		1,335	167										
3	/o/			671	106	132	18	121	25	326	41	92	22
	/ɑɪ/			632	56			169	28	463	28		
	/ɒ/			32	5			32	5				
oy		152	32										
1	/ɔ̇/			152	32			51	6	101	26		
ph		108	60										
1	/f/			108	60	80	42	6	5	22	13		
pn		3	1										
1	/n/			3	1	3	1						

pp	/p/	362	117										
1				362	117	188	63	21	8	153	46		
ps		2	2										
1	/s/			2	2	2	2						
pt		9	2										
1	/t/			9	2			1	1	8	1		
re		8	1										
1	/r/			8	1					8	1		
rh		5	5										
1	/r/			5	5	5	5						
rr		400	143										
1	/r/			400	143	99	36	31	11	270	96		
rt		1	1										
1	/r/			1	1					1	1		
sc		65	39										
3	/s/			55	33	35	19			20	14		
	/z/			8	5	7	4			1	1		
	/ʃ/			2	1	2	1						
sh		1,178	278										
1	/ʃ/			1,178	278	853	151	78	24	245	102		2	1

Grapheme	Phoneme	Grapheme totals Oc	Grapheme totals It	Phoneme totals Oc	Phoneme totals It	Initial Oc	Initial It	Medial Oc	Medial It	Final Oc	Final It	Syllabic Oc	Syllabic It
si		103	39										
2	/ʒ/			81	24	34	14			47	10		
	/ʃ/			22	15	22	15						
sl		5	3										
1	/l/			5	3	3	2			2	1		
ss		1,246	367										
3	/s/			1,156	342	118	45	79	26	959	271		
	/ʃ/			65	14	15	7			50	7		
	/z/			25	11	24	10			1	1		
st		35	17										
1	/s/			35	17			1	1	34	16		
sw		34	6										
1	/s/			34	6	34	6						
te		4	2										
1	/ʗ/			4	2	4	2						
th		6,839	325										
2	/ħ/			5,447	113	4,106	48	14	7	1,327	58		
	/ꜧ/			1,392	212	872	102	44	10	476	100		

ti		1,416	428										
2	/ʃ/			1,360	418	1,157	379			203	39		
	/ċ/			56	10	56	10						
tt		751	152										
1	/t/			751	152	122	28	2	1	627	123		
tw		146	1										
1	/t/			146	1	146	1						
ua		22	11										
2	/ɑ/			15	8			15	8				
	/a/			7	3			7	3				
ue		162	36										
6	/ɯ̇/			53	14			8	4	45	10		
	/ɯ/			44	5			2	2	42	3		
	/u/			40	9	19	4	2	2	2	1	17	2
	/e/			21	5			21	5				
	/ɐ/			2	1			2	1				
	/ə/			2	2	1	1	1	1				
ui		126	33										
5	/i/			87	16	1	1	86	15				
	/ɯ̇/			22	5			22	5				
	/ɯ/			15	10			15	10				
	/ɛ/			1	1					1	1		
	/ȧ/			1	1			1	1				

Grapheme	Phoneme	Grapheme totals Oc	Grapheme totals It	Phoneme totals Oc	Phoneme totals It	Initial Oc	Initial It	Medial Oc	Medial It	Final Oc	Final It	Syllabic Oc	Syllabic It
uo		1	1										
1	/ə/			1	1	1	1						
uy		37	6										
1	/ȧ/			37	6			2	2	35	4		
ve		12	2										
1	/v/			12	2					12	2		
wh		377	9										
1	/h/			377	9	377	9						
wr		122	22										
1	/r/			122	22	122	22						
ye		2	2										
1	/ȧ/			2	2			1	1	1	1		
zz		10	7										
1	/z/			10	7					10	7		
Simple digraph totals													
103	168	42,651	7,586										

				All other spellings							
a-e		3,697	549								
6	/ꬱ/			1,918	355	46	19	1,870	334	2	2
	/a/			665	23	3	2	662	21		
	/ɑ/			661	22	549	2	112	20		
	/i/			296	94	169	53	127	41		
	/ə/			148	51	47	22	101	29		
	/ɔ/			9	4			9	4		
a-ue		2	1								
1	/ꬱ/			2	1			2	1		
ai-e		31	12								
2	/ꬱ/			29	11	6	3	23	8		
	/ȧ/			2	1	2	1				
aigh		22	5								
1	/ꬱ/			22	5			22	5		
au-e		163	9								
3	/ɔ/			161	7			161	7		
	/ꬱ/			1	1			1	1		
	/o/			1	1			1	1		
augh		32	8								
1	/ɔ/			32	8			27	6	5	2

Grapheme	Phoneme	Grapheme totals Oc	Grapheme totals It	Phoneme totals Oc	Phoneme totals It	Initial Oc	Initial It	Medial Oc	Medial It	Final Oc	Final It	Syllabic Oc	Syllabic It
awe		1	1										
1	/ɔ/			1	1							1	1
aye		1	1										
1	/ɑ/			1	1			1	1				
cht		1	1										
1	/t/			1	1					1	1		
é		1	1										
1	/ɑ/			1	1					1	1		
e′e		1	1										
1	/ɛ/			1	1	1	1						
e-e		1,808	197										
5	/e/			530	96	314	36	216	60				
	/ɑ/			464	24	1	1	463	23				
	/ɛ/			444	46	27	5	417	41				
	/ə/			360	27			360	27				
	/i/			10	4	3	1	7	3				

e-ue		7	4										
1	/e/			7	4	3	1	4	3				
ea-e		176	28										
2	/ɛ/			175	27	10	3	165	24				
	/ə/			1	1			1	1				
ea-ue		5	1										
1	/ɛ/			5	1			5	1				
eau		30	4										
2	/i̇u/			24	3					24	3		
	/o/			6	1					6	1		
ee-e		10	6										
1	/ɛ/			10	6			10	6				
ei-e		64	11										
1	/ɛ/			64	11			64	11				
eigh		139	23										
2	/ɑ/			82	19	10	4	47	7	25	8		
	/ɑ̇/			57	4	33	1	6	2			18	1
eu-e		1	1										
1	/i̇u/			1	1			1	1				

Grapheme	Phoneme	Grapheme totals Oc	Grapheme totals It	Phoneme totals Oc	Phoneme totals It	Initial Oc	Initial It	Medial Oc	Medial It	Final Oc	Final It	Syllabic Oc	Syllabic It
½ew		2	2										
2	/y/			1	1	1	1						
	/u/			1	1					1	1		
eye		55	4										
1	/ȧ/			55	4	36	2					19	2
hau		3	1										
1	/ɔ/			3	1	3	1						
hou		55	4										
1	/ɑɪ/			55	4	55	4						
i-e		2,402	489										
3	/ȧ/			1,802	324	78	25	1,724	299				
	/i/			537	151	58	22	479	129				
	/ɛ/			63	14	1	1	62	13				
i-ue		4	3										
1	/ɛ/			4	3			4	3				
½i-o		16	6										
2	/ə/			8	3	8	3						
	/ȧ/			8	3							8	3

ia-e		7	2								
1	/i/			7	2	7	2				
ie-e		87	14								
1	/ɛ/			87	14			87	14		
ieu		2	2								
1	/ɨɯ/			2	2					2	2
iew		43	8								
1	/ɨɯ/			43	8			9	4	34	4
igh		546	74								
1	/ȧ/			546	74			447	63	99	11
o-e		2,014	268								
6	/o/			1,199	183	3	2	1,193	180	3	1
	/ʊ/			565	34			565	34		
	/ɯ/			112	15			112	15		
	/ə/			60	5	1	1	59	4		
	/ɔ/			43	10			43	10		
	/ɒ/			35	21			35	21		
o-o		5	3								
1	/ə/			5	3			5	3		

Grapheme	Phoneme	Grapheme totals		Phoneme totals		Initial		Medial		Final		Syllabic	
		Oc	It	Oc	It	Oc	It	Oc	It	Oc	It	Oc	It
o-ue		20	8										
3	/ɒ/			13	5			13	5				
	/ʊ/			6	2			6	2				
	/o/			1	1			1	1				
½o-e		900	10										
2	/w/			450	5	450	5						
	/ʊ/			450	5			450	5				
oa-e		7	4										
1	/o/			7	4			7	4				
oeu		1	1										
1	/ɯ/			1	1					1	1		
oi-e		30	7										
1	/ɔ̇i/			30	7			30	7				
½oi		2	2										
2	/w/			1	1			1	1				
	/ɑ/			1	1					1	1		

oo-e		11	6										
1	/ɯ/			11	6	1	1	10	5				
ou-e		273	48										
3	/ɑɪ/			194	40	1	1	96	19	97	20		
	/o/			56	4			56	4				
	/ɯ/			23	4			23	4				
ough		318	24										
4	/ɔ/			152	9			152	9				
	/ɯ/			92	2					92	2		
	/o/			65	7					60	5	5	2
	/ɑɪ/			9	6			7	4	2	2		
owe		2	1										
1	/o/			2	1							2	1
pph		1	1										
1	/f/			1	1					1	1		
½re		26	20										
2	/r/			13	10			6	4	7	6		
	/ə/			13	10			13	10				
rps		5	1										
1	/r/			5	1					5	1		
rrh		1	1										
1	/r/			1	1	1	1						

Grapheme	Phoneme	Grapheme totals Oc	Grapheme totals It	Phoneme totals Oc	Phoneme totals It	Initial Oc	Initial It	Medial Oc	Medial It	Final Oc	Final It	Syllabic Oc	Syllabic It
sci		17	5										
1	/ʃ/			17	5	15	4			2	1		
ssi		77	28										
1	/ʃ/			77	28					77	28		
tch		85	36										
1	/ċ/			85	36			12	4	73	32		
the		7,310	1										
1	/ŧə/			7,310	1							7,310	1
u-e		690	200										
6	/u/			297	78	56	12	241	66				
	/iɯ/			248	81			248	81				
	/ɯ/			79	19			79	19				
	/i/			30	3	30	3						
	/ʊ/			19	9			19	9				
	/ə/			17	10	5	2	12	8				
u-ue		1	1										
1	/ʊ/			1	1			1	1				

½u		714	295										
3	/y/			357	148	357	148						
	/u/			257	117			12	5	245	112		
	/ɯ/			100	30			39	9	61	21		
½u-e		364	36										
3	/y/			182	18	182	18						
	/ɯ/			125	9			97	8	28	1		
	/u/			57	9			57	9				
ual		1	1										
1	/l/			1	1	1	1						
½ue		137	15										
3	/y/			68	7	68	7						
	/ɯ/			51	4			5	2	46	2		
	/u/			18	4			16	3	2	1		
ugh		1	1										
1	/u/			1	1							1	1
ui-e		7	6										
2	/ȧ/			6	5			6	5				
	/ɯ/			1	1			1	1				
½wh		2,718	96										
2	/w/			1,359	48			1,359	48				
	/h/			1,359	48	1,359	48						

Grapheme	Phoneme	Grapheme totals Oc	Grapheme totals It	Phoneme totals Oc	Phoneme totals It	Initial Oc	Initial It	Medial Oc	Medial It	Final Oc	Final It	Syllabic Oc	Syllabic It
½x		1,216	390										
6	/k/			510	165			507	164	3	1		
	/s/			495	162			71	10	424	152		
	/g/			104	31			103	30	1	1		
	/z/			103	30					103	30		
	/ʃ/			3	1	3	1						
	/ʒ/			1	1	1	1						
½xi		25	9										
2	/k/			13	5	1	1			12	4		
	/ʃ/			12	4	12	4						
y–e		31	11										
1	/ȧ/			31	11			31	11				

All other spellings totals

64	117	26,424	3,009	

Summary

Graphemes	Phonemes	Grapheme totals Oc	It	Percent of all graphemes	Phonemes/Graphemes	: Ratio	Occurrences/Items	: Ratio
Single letters								
26	77	295,306	53,734	81.0	77 / 26	3.0	295,306 / 53,734	5.5
Simple digraphs								
103	168	42,651	7,586	11.7	168 / 103	1.6	42,651 / 7,586	5.6
*All other spellings**								
64	117	26,424	3,009	7.3	117 / 64	1.8	26,424 / 3,009	8.8
TOTALS								
193	362	364,381	64,329	100.0	362 / 193	1.9	364,381 / 64,329	5.7

* Includes *the*

Table 7 Distribution of spellings by frequency of occurrences

Grouped by form of grapheme

Occurrences		*Category totals* Oc		*Per-cent*	*Cumu-lative totals* Oc		*Per-cent*
Over 10,000		11		3.0	11		3.0
(4 over 20,000)	Single letter		11			11	
	Simple digraph		—			—	
	All other		—			—	
10,000 to 1,001		49		13.6	60		16.6
	Single letter		29			40	
	Simple digraph		14			14	
	All other		6			6	
1,000 to 101		92		25.4	152		42.0
	Single letter		18			58	
	Simple digraph		45			59	
	All other		29			35	
100 to 11		103		28.4	255		70.4
	Single letter		8			66	
	Simple digraph		57			116	
	All other		38			73	
10 to 1		107		29.6	362		100.0
	Single letter		11			77	
	Simple digraph		52			168	
	All other		44			117	

Table 8 Comparative dispersion of spellings

Grouped by form of grapheme

		Totals		Graphemes for Consonant phonemes	Graphemes for Vowel phonemes	Percent of *Hws*
Identified by *How we spell!* (1968, 1969) 41-phoneme basis		561				100.0
	Single letter		92	51	41	
	Simple digraph		260	114	146	
	All other		209	52	157	
Reported in Tables 5 and 6 this study 41+*the* phoneme basis		362				65.0
	Single letter		77	41	36	
	Simple digraph		168	78	90	
	All other		117	26	90	
Reported in Tables 8 and 7 Hanna study 52-phoneme basis		378				(not com-par-able)
	Single letter		97	45	52	
	Simple digraph		182	89	93	
	All other		99	10	89	
Hanna data reduced to 41-phoneme basis		325				58.5
	Single letter		79	43	36	
	Simple digraph		160	78	82	
	All other		86	9	77	
Reported *both* in this study and Hanna study		270				48.5
	Single letter		74	38	36	
	Simple digraph		129	64	65	
	All other		67	4	63	

Chapter 6

Practical applications

Whatever judgment may be passed on this study as a contribution to pure scholarship, its justification, so far as I am concerned, lies in its immediate practical application to mitigating the impact of our present English spelling on the most pressing problem of elementary education, learning to read and write; and in its further contribution to eliminating eventually that particular obstructive factor, thru spelling reform. I have suggested in the preface a few immediate applications of these data, but as I have discussed elsewhere,[1] at some length, several important aspects of the larger problem, this chapter will confine itself to a few suggestions as to how best to make use of these data, and one example of applying them to a detailed appraisal of a phonemic notation.

How much weight to give to a particular frequency in applying the data of these tables to practical purposes is a critically important question. It may help some people to visualize the total corpus investigated — 100,000 running words, about 143,000 syllables, consisting of slightly over 364,000 phonemes, spelled by just over 438,000 letters — as a 250-page book with 400 words to the page (rather small type), or 300 pages of manuscript, typed double-spaced on ordinary 8½ x 11 inch paper with elite (12-pitch) type, or 360 pages if typed with pica (10-pitch) type. Table 7, showing the distribution of spellings by frequency of occur-

[1] Dewey, *English spelling: Roadblock to reading* (in press).

rences should be helpful in this connection. It is obvious that a spelling which occurs over 10,000 times, or at least once in an average line of print or typing is in the top level of importance. It is no less obvious that a spelling which occurs 10 times or less, or once in 25 pages, rates a distinctly lower priority. At the level of 100 occurrences, or an average of once in 2½ pages, a particular spelling would seem to call for serious consideration. The twilight zone, therefore, appears to lie between 100 and 10 occurrences.

The most significant and distinctive contribution of this study is the provision of trustworthy data, not heretofore available in any complete or comparable form based on adequate research, on the relative frequency of *occurrences* of particular phoneme-grapheme correspondences on the printed page. Data on the number of *items* (different syllables or words) exhibiting a particular phoneme-grapheme correspondence, as exhaustively investigated by Hanna, are also, however, significant; and data on occurrences are often more significant when coupled with the number of items represented. Most data regarding particular phonemes or graphemes or phoneme-grapheme correspondences will therefore usually be stated in the form x/y, where x is the total number of occurrences and y the number of different items involved — per 100,000 running words always understood. Thus, on the first page of Table 5, the phoneme /t/ is reported as occurring 29,609/4,496 times; the grapheme *tt* for /t/ as occurring 751/152 times. This form of statement will be used without further explanation from this point on.

In general, the data of Table 5, Spellings of sounds, apply most directly to the problems of writing, more particularly spelling, whereas the data of Table 6, Pronunciations of spellings, apply more directly to the problems of reading. Their greatest usefulness, however, in connection with such purposes as suggested in the preface, "to select for earliest introduction or greatest emphasis, in teaching materials, those phoneme-grapheme correspondences which will occur most frequently *and/or* with the least irregularity," will usually involve employment of both tables in conjunction. For example:

Examining the first grapheme under each phoneme in Table 5 reveals that *s*, which is the most frequent grapheme for /s/ (12,822/2,974), is at the same time the most frequent grapheme for /z/ (10,695/1,902) — both high frequency occurrences. Continuing thru the vowel phonemes reveals that *a* is the most frequent grapheme not only for the short sound /a/ and the name sound /ɑ/, but also for /ɑ/ and /ə/. Likewise, *e* is the most frequent grapheme both for /e/ and /ɛ/; *i* is the most frequent grapheme both for /i/ and /ȧ/; *o*, like *a*, is the most frequent grapheme for 4 phonemes, /ɒ/, /ɔ/, /o/, and /ɯ/; and *u* is the most frequent grapheme both for /ʋ/ and /iɯ/. Table 6 brings together, in order of frequency, 8 phonemes represented by the grapheme *a*, but only Table 5 brings out clearly the fact that for 4 of these 8 phonemes *a* is the most frequent representation. Obviously, any notation purporting to be phonemic, which builds on the Roman alphabet, must settle for *one* phoneme-grapheme correspondence for each of these single letters; whether for the most frequent occurrence (e.g., *a* for /a/, not /ɑ/) or for the most unmistakable (e.g., *z*, not *s*, for /z/); and find acceptable symbolizations for the rest.

Substantially the same problem arises with familiar digraphs. Among consonants, *th* is the most frequent grapheme both for the unvoiced phoneme /ꞁ/ and for the far more frequently occurring voiced phoneme /ħ/. Among the vowels, the digraph *ea* (2,205/432) is most frequently pronounced /ɛ/, but is also the most frequently employed digraph for /ɑ/, /e/, and /ə/; *ou* (3,761/383) is most frequently pronounced /ɑɩ/, but is also the most frequently employed digraph for /ʋ/, /u/, and /ɯ/; and *ow* (1,335/167) is the most frequently employed digraph both for /o/ and /ɑɩ/. Also, *oo* (862/155), altho not the most frequent digraph for any sound, occurs with almost equal frequency as the second commonest digraph for both /ɯ/ and /u/. It is problems such as these, among others, which must be taken into account in constructing or appraising a phonemic notation of the standardizing (no-new-letter) type.

A frequency-oriented analysis of WES

Table 9 presents what is probably the most thoroly researched no-new-letter phonemic notation for English now before the public: WES, the World English Spelling of the Simpler Spelling Association, which, as a spelling reform proposal has a history of evolution thru international study and conference going back at least 60 years.[2] The form here presented is the i.t.m. version, which, on the basis of i.t.a. experience, incorporates three significant departures from one sound, one symbol writing — doubled consonants, where T.O. has doubled consonants; *c* as well as *k* for the /k/ phoneme, where T.O. has *c;* and *y* for final schwi, where T.O. has *y* — to better adapt it for use as an initial teaching medium, for which maximum compatibility with T.O., to facilitate the eventual transition to T.O., is an important qualification.

Table 10 presents a frequency-oriented analysis of WES which distinguishes the spelling reform and i.t.m. versions. Obviously there is much more to devising the most efficient no-new-letter notation for English than merely considering the relative frequency of spellings and pronunciations. The very similar New Spelling of the Simplified Spelling Society takes a book of 130 pages to present and justify its decisions.[3] Elsewhere I have discussed at some length the more important of the further factors involved.[4] Nevertheless, the proportion of T.O. phoneme-grapheme correspondences retained on the printed page is the acid test, and the 74% ratio for the spelling reform version of WES and 79% for the slightly modified i.t.m. version exceeds any acceptably phonemic no-new-letter notation of which I have knowledge.

[2] Appendix E gives a complete summary of the spelling reform version of WES. For a fuller account of its history, see Dewey, *English spelling: Roadblock to reading* (in press), Ch. 3.

[3] Ripman, *et al., New Spelling,* 6th ed. (1948).

[4] Dewey, *English spelling: Roadblock to reading* (in press).

Table 9 World English Spelling (WES) — i. t. m. version

Consonants	*As in*	*Vowels and diphthongs*	*As in*
p	*p*ay, ha*pp*y, ca*p*	**a**	*a*t, m*a*n; *a*sk; *a*bout, dat*a*
b	*b*ay, ru*bb*er, ca*b*	**aa**	*a*lms, f*a*ther, b*ah*; (ask)
t	*t*own, le*tt*er, bi*t*	**ar**	*ar*my, m*ar*ket, f*ar*
d	*d*own, la*dd*er, bi*d*	**e**	*e*dge, m*e*n, s*ai*d, h*ea*d, *a*ny
c	*c*ame, a*cc*ount, publi*c*; ba*c*k	**ae**	*a*ge, m*ai*n, s*ay*, gr*ea*t
k	*k*eep, wee*k*; bac*k*; e*x*pect; *q*uite	**aer**	*air*, c*are*, th*eir*
g	*g*ame, ra*gg*ed, ba*g*; e*x*act	**i**	*i*t, h*i*m, pr*e*tty, g*i*ve
f	*f*ast, o*ff*ice, *ph*otogra*ph*, sa*f*e	**ee**	*ea*ch, h*e*r*e*, s*ee*, b*e*
v	*v*ast, ne*v*er, sa*v*e	**o**	*o*n, b*o*ther, n*o*t; w*a*s, wh*a*t
thh	*th*ought, no*th*ing, bo*th*	**au**	*au*thor, l*aw*, *a*ll, w*a*ter, *ou*ght
th	*th*at, ra*th*er, wi*th*	**or**	*or*der, n*or*th, f*or*; st*or*y, m*ore*
s	*s*eal, le*ss*on, *c*ity, ra*c*e, ba*s*e	**u**	*u*p, *o*ther, b*u*t, s*o*m*e*, t*ou*ch
z	*z*eal, pu*zz*le, i*s*, rai*s*e, si*z*e	**oe**	*o*ld, n*o*t*e*, g*oe*s, s*o*, c*oa*l, sh*ow*
sh	*sh*all, pre*ss*ure, na*ti*on, wi*sh*	**uu**	f*u*ll, s*u*r*e*, sh*ou*ld, g*oo*d
zh	*j*abot, plea*s*ure, vi*si*on, rouge	**oo**	f*oo*l, m*o*v*e*, gr*ou*p, r*u*l*e*, t*oo*
ch	*ch*eck, *ch*ur*ch*, wa*tch*	**ie**	*i*c*e*, t*ie*, k*i*nd, m*i*ght, b*y*
j	*j*ust, *g*eneral, sta*g*e, *j*u*dg*e	**ou**	*ou*t, p*ou*nd, n*ow*, b*ough*
m	*m*ight, co*mm*on, the*m*	**oi**	*oi*l, p*oi*nt, b*oy*
n	*n*ight, di*nn*er, the*n*	**ue**	*u*s*e*, m*u*sic, d*ue*, f*ew*
ng	thi*ng*, lo*ng*, goi*ng*, si*n*gle	**er**	furth*er*, coll*ar*, mot*or*, murm*ur*
nk	thi*nk*, ba*nk*, u*nc*le, a*nk*le	**ur**	f*ur*ther, h*er*, *ear*ly, f*ir*st, w*or*k
l	*l*ate, fe*ll*ow, dea*l*		
r	*r*ate, ma*rr*ied, dea*r*		
w	*w*et, for*w*ard, *o*ne, q*u*ick		
wh	*wh*ich, every*wh*ere		
y	*y*et, be*y*ond, mill*i*on; an*y*; *y*ou		
h	*h*ad, be*h*ind, *wh*o		

For teaching purposes, use only lower-case letter forms.

Separate by a dot successive letters which might otherwise be read as a digraph —

short.hand, mis.hap, en.gaej, man.kiend
gae.ety, ree.elect, hie.est, loe.er, influu.ens, pou.er, emploi.ee

Table 10 Percent of T.O. phoneme-grapheme correspondences retained by WES (Spelling reform version)

Consonants

Phoneme	WES grapheme	Rank in Table 5	WES grapheme in Table 5 Oc	WES grapheme in Table 5 It	Phoneme totals Table 5 Oc	Phoneme totals Table 5 It	Percent Oc	Percent It
/**p**/	p	1	7,276	1,850	7,638	1,967	95.2	94.1
/**b**/	b	1	6,686	1,130	6,721	1,152	99.5	97.8
/**t**/	t	1	24,998	4,122	26,609	4,496	93.8	91.5
/**d**/	d	1	14,285	2,723	15,723	3,052	90.7	89.3
/**k**/	k	2	1,854	343	10,010	2,680	18.5	12.8
/**g**/	g	1	2,616	560	2,794	636	93.7	88.0
/**f**/	f	1	6,117	954	6,889	1,131	88.9	84.2
/**v**/	v	1	4,403	899	8,417	905	52.3	99.3
/**ħ**/	thh	0	0	0	1,396	213	0	0
/**ɦ**/	th	1	5,447	113	5,447	113	100.0	100.0
/**s**/	s	1	12,822	2,974	17,081	4,162	75.2	71.6
/**z**/	z	2	247	107	11,089	2,063	2.2	5.2
/**ʃ**/	sh	2	1,178	278	3,045	850	38.7	32.7
/**ʒ**/	zh	0	0	0	170	52	0	0
/**ȼ**/	ch	1	1,457	215	1,931	348	75.4	61.8
/**j**/	j	2	414	111	1,582	492	26.1	22.6
/**m**/	m	1	10,049	1,727	10,281	1,820	97.8	94.8
/**n**/	n	1	25,727	4,168	26,982	4,411	95.4	94.5
/**ŋ**/	ng	1	3,164	911	3,550	1,035	89.2	88.2
	n(k)	2	385	123	"	"	10.8	11.8
/**l**/	l	1	10,288	2,621	13,940	3,274	73.7	81.6
/**r**/	r	1	24,911	5,237	25,471	5,424	97.8	96.5
/**w**/	w	1	5,527	380	7,741	553	71.4	68.7
	w(h)	2	1,359	48	"	"	17.5	8.7
/**y**/	y	1	1,507	40	2,260	250	66.7	16.0
/**h**/	h	1	5,023	427	6,759	484	74.3	88.3
	(w)h	2	1,359	48	"	"	20.1	9.9
Consonant subtotals			179,159	32,109	223,526	41,563	79.5	77.3

Table 10 (continued)

Vowels

Phoneme	WES grapheme	Rank in Table 5	Table 5 Oc	Table 5 It	Phoneme totals Table 5 Oc	Phoneme totals Table 5 It	Percent Oc	Percent It
/a/	a	1	13,174	1,536	13,852	1,565	95.0	98.1
/ɑ/	aa	8	3	3	1,831	332	0.2	0.3
	a(r)	1	1,052	275	"	"	57.5	83.7
/e/	e	1	10,987	2,941	12,709	3,172	86.3	93.0
/ɑ/	ae	0	0	0	7,770	1,446	0	0
/i/	i	1	20,276	3,807	29,283	5,962	69.2	63.8
/ɛ/	ee	3	1,158	175	7,114	834	16.3	21.0
/ɒ/	o	1	9,150	1,022	10,521	1,103	86.9	92.6
/ɔ/	au	6	69	38	4,691	442	1.5	8.6
	o(r)	(1)	2,078	102	"	"	44.2	17.2
/ʋ/	u	1	3,768	797	6,273	1,118	60.0	71.3
/o/	oe	9	38	13	6,091	1,188	0.6	1.1
/u/	uu	0	0	0	2,577	466	0	0
/ɯ/	oo	3	430	88	6,051	322	7.1	27.3
/ə/					15,024	3,273	*	*
	a	1	5,602	1,105	"	"	37.3	33.8
	e	2	5,027	1,051	"	"	33.4	32.1
	o	3	2,901	787	"	"	19.2	24.1
	u	4	369	107	"	"	2.5	3.3
	i	6	330	57	"	"	2.2	1.7
/ɑ̇/	ie	5	153	49	5,961	859	2.6	5.7
/ɔ̇/	oi	1	165	66	347	105	47.7	62.7
/ɑu/	ou	1	1,422	150	2,312	256	61.6	58.7
/iɯ/	ue	4	53	14	1,138	322	4.7	4.4
Vowel subtotals			78,205	14,181	133,545	22,765	58.7	62.2

*Total percent of WES graphemes for schwa: 94.6 (Oc), 95.0 (It)

"Wordsigns"

		WES graphemes Table 5		Phoneme totals Table 5		Percent	
		Oc	It	Oc	It	Oc	It
(1)	th(e)	7,310	1	7,310	1		
	(th)e	7,310	1	7,310	3		
(2)	(t)o	2,924	1				
(3)	a(10%)	212	1				
Wordsign subtotals		17,756	4	14,620	4		

Actually the 3 words listed above are not arbitrary "wordsigns" but merely extension of the general rule for representing schwa — to retain any single vowel letter of T.O. — to the usual unstressed pronunciations of 3 of the most frequently occurring words of English. To facilitate reference to the basic data of Tables 5 and 6, however, they are here listed separately.

(1) The graphemes and phonemes for the consonant and vowels of the SSA wordsign *the* (see discussion in Ch. 2, p. 13) are not included in the preceding tables.

(2) The vowel grapheme for the word *to* is not included under schwa above.

(3) 10 % of the occurrences of the grapheme for the word *a* (see discussion of assumptions regarding pronunciations of *the* and *a* in Ch. 2, p. 13) are not included under schwa above.

Table 10 (continued)
Additional percent of T.O. graphemes corresponding to i.t.m. version of WES

Pho- neme	WES graphemes	Rank in Table 5	Table 5 Oc	Table 5 It	Phoneme totals Table 5 Oc	Phoneme totals Table 5 It	Percent Oc	Percent It
Doubled consonants								
/p/	pp	2	362	117	7,638	1,967	47.3	5.9
/b/	bb	2	35	22	6,721	1,152	0.5	1.9
/t/	tt	2	751	152	26,609	4,496	2.8	3.4
/d/	dd	4	138	41	15,723	3,052	0.9	1.3
/g/	gg	3	70	42	2,794	636	2.5	6.6
/f/	ff	2	510	102	6,889	1,131	7.4	9.0
/s/	ss	3	1,156	342	17,081	4,162	6.8	8.2
/z/	zz	5	10	7	11,089	2,063	0.1	0.3
/m/	mm	2	182	70	10,281	1,820	1.8	3.8
/n/	nn	4	249	54	26,982	4,411	0.9	1.2
/l/	ll	2	2,519	342	13,940	3,274	18.1	10.4
/r/	rr	2	400	143	25,471	5,424	1.6	2.6
Subtotals			6,382	1,434	171,218*	33,588	3.7	4.3
c as well as *k*								
/k/					10,010	2,680		
	c	1	6,403	1,775	"	"	64.0	66.2
	ck	4	452	151	"	"	4.5	5.6
	cc	6	144	45	"	"	1.4	1.7
Subtotals			6,999	1,971	10,010*	2,680	69.9	73.5
y for unstressed final **/i/**								
/i/					29,283	5,962		
	y	2	3,986	835			13.6	14.0
Subtotals			3,986	835	29,283*	5,962	13.6	14.0
th for unvoiced as well as voiced sounds, unless conflicting								
/ꝧ/					1,392	213		
	th	1	1,384	211			99.9	99.0
Subtotals			1,384	211	1,392*	213	99.9	99.0
Additional TOTALS for i.t.m. WES			18,751	4,451	371,691	64,332	5.0	6.9

* All phoneme totals have been included under spelling reform WES. They are here repeated only to substantiate percentages.

Summary

	WES graphemes		Phoneme totals		Percent	
	Oc	It	Oc	It	Oc	It
Consonant subtotals	179,159	32,109	223,526	41,563	79.5	77.3
Vowel subtotals	78,205	14,181	133,545	22,765	58.7	62.2
Consonant & vowel subtotals	257,364	46,290	357,071	64,328	72.2	72.0
Wordsign subtotals	17,756	4	14,620	4		
TOTALS for spelling reform WES	275,120	46,294	371,691	64,332	74.1	72.1
Additional percent of T.O. graphemes for i.t.m. WES	18,751	4,451	"	"	5.0	6.9
TOTALS for i.t.m. WES	293,871	50,745	371,691	64,332	79.1	79.0

Chapter 7

General summary

Summarizing the more important findings of this study:

1. *For comparison, Hws* identified in the *American College Dictionary:*

561 spellings of 41 sounds; an average of 13.7 spellings per sound.[1]

This study found, in 10,119 different words, making up 100,000 running words of well-diversified connected matter:

362 graphemes for 41 phonemes (plus *the*); an average of 8.6 graphemes per phoneme (Table 5). Of these, 255 occurred oftener than 10 times (Table 7).

The Hanna study, reducing its data to the same 41-phoneme basis, found in 17,310 different words, representing 4½ million running words:

325 graphemes for 41 phonemes; an average of 7.9 graphemes per phoneme (Ch. 1, p. 5).

The Hanna study provides no data on *occurrences;* only on *items*.

2. *For comparison, Hws* found

561 pronunciations for 280 different spellings; an average of 2.0 pronunciations per spelling.[2]

[1] Dewey, *English spelling: Roadblock to reading* (in press), Appendix A.
[2] *Ibid.*, Appendix B.

This study found
362 pronunciations for 193 different spellings; an average of 1.9 pronunciations per spelling (Table 6).

The Hanna study found (on a 41-phoneme basis)
325 pronunciations for 160 different spellings; an average of 2.0 pronunciations per spelling (Ch. 1, p. 5).

3. Found both in this study and the Hanna study were
270 spellings (Table 8). This study found that, of these, 218 occurred oftener than 10 times (Ch. 5, p. 50).

4. Because the phonemic-graphemic structure of T.O. is the one datum common to all theories about or approaches to the reading problem, both the phonemic data of *RF/Sounds* and the graphemic data of this study are of inescapable significance.

5. These data should be of particular value in devising, applying, and/or testing a phonemic notation as an initial teaching medium or proposals for spelling reform, the criteria for which are by no means the same.[3]

As in my earlier study, *RF/Sounds*, I have been at pains to select and report the observed data with complete objectivity, without regard to the particular purposes for which I myself find them of greatest interest and value. I hope that this objectivity may lead, as it did with the earlier study, to a considerably wider range of usefulness than originally anticipated.[4]

[3] *Ibid.*, Ch. 6, Initial teaching orthographies
[4] Dewey, *RF/Sounds* (1950), p. x.

Appendix A Grapheme-phoneme correspondences (Pronunciations of spellings) On a 52-symbol basis

Arranged from Hanna Tables 7 and 8,
Phoneme-grapheme correspondences (Spellings of sounds)

Graphemes are arranged in 3 groups:
single letters, simple digraphs, all other spellings.

In each group, graphemes are arranged alphabetically.

Under each grapheme,
phonemes are arranged by frequency (of items).

Percent signifies that of the different items (syllables or words) containing that phoneme, that proportion are spelled by that grapheme. These percentages, which appear in the Hanna tables, are there cumulated to 100 % under each phoneme. They cannot be cumulated here, since each is the quotient of a different dividend and divisor.

The SSA phonemic alphabet distinguishes only 17 vowel phonemes, as compared with the 22 vowel symbols distinguished by the Hanna notation. In this table, the supernumerary distinctions are indicated as follows:

′ SSA, in agreement with the Revised Scientific Alphabet used in Appendix C, does not distinguish /E2/ from /E/, /E5/ from /ə/, or /O5/ from /O3/.

″ SSA combines /A2/ with /A/, as do Pitman's i.t.a. and WES.

* SSA combines /U2/ with /ə/, as do *Webster's Third New International Dictionary*, *Webster's Seventh New Collegiate Dictionary*, etc.

Single letters

Grapheme	Phoneme: Hanna symbol	Phoneme: SSA symbol	Frequency	Percent
A	/A3/	/**a**/	4,192	96.58
10	/ə/	/**ə**/	1,438	23.91
	/A/	/**ɑ**/	1,002	44.57
	/A5/	/**ɑ**/	518	89.31
	/E5/	/**ə**/′	168	7.74
	/O2/	/**ɔ**/	165	21.51
	/E3/	/**e**/	94	2.57
	/O3/	/**ɒ**/	80	4.80
	/A2/	/**ɑ**/″	64	29.09
	/I3/	/**i**/	4	.05
B	/B/	/**b**/	2,239	97.22
1				

Grapheme	Phoneme Hanna symbol	Phoneme SSA symbol	Frequency	Percent
C	/K/	/**k**/	3,452	73.25
4	/S/	/**s**/	1,067	16.86
	/SH/	/**ʃ**/	38	2.47
	/CH/	/**ċ**/	2	.35
D	/D/	/**d**/	3,611	97.83
2	/J/	/**j**/	32	3.25
E	/E3/	/**e**/	3,316	90.94
11	/E/	/**ɛ**/	1,765	69.64
	/E5/	/**ə**/′	1,666	76.77
	/ə/	/**ə**/	763	12.68
	/U2/	/**ə**/*	313	39.77
	/E2/	/**ɛ**/′	64	32.32
	/A/	/**ɑ**/	16	.71
	/A5/	/**ɑ**/	5	.86
	/I3/	/**i**/	5	.06
	/A2/	/**ɑ**/″	4	1.81
	/Y/	/**y**/	1	.83
F	/F/	/**f**/	1,580	78.25
2	/V/	/**v**/	3	.20
G	/G/	/**g**/	1,178	88.04
3	/J/	/**j**/	647	65.88
	/ZH/	/**ʒ**/	15	14.70
H	/H/	/**h**/	762	97.94
1				
I	/I3/	/**i**/	5,346	68.40
8	/ə/	/**ə**/	1,347	22.40
	/I/	/**ἀ**/	554	37.38
	/U2/	/**ə**/*	104	13.21
	/Y/	/**y**/	66	55.00
	/E/	/**ɛ**/	38	1.49
	/E5/	/**ə**/′	8	.36
	/E2/	/**ɛ**/′	3	1.51
J	/J/	/**j**/	218	22.24
1				

Grapheme	Phoneme Hanna symbol	Phoneme SSA symbol	Frequency	Percent
K 1	/K/	/**k**/	601	12.75
L 1	/L/	/**l**/	4,894	90.81
M 2	/M/	/**m**/	3,302	94.31
	/M1/	/**m**/′	97	100.00
N 2	/N/	/**n**/	7,452	97.33
	/NG/	/**ŋ**/	251	40.81
O 11	/O/	/**o**/	1,876	72.51
	/ə/	/**ə**/	1,611	26.79
	/O3/	/**ɒ**/	1,558	93.74
	/O2/	/**ɔ**/	312	40.67
	/E5/	/**ə**/′	268	12.35
	/O5/	/**ɒ**/′	123	96.85
	/U3/	/**u**/	112	7.94
	/U2/	/**ə**/*	53	6.73
	/O6/	/**ɯ**/	37	8.16
	/O7/	/**u**/	17	4.61
	/I3/	/**i**/	1	.01
P 1	/P/	/**p**/	3,296	95.56
Q 1	/K/	/**k**/	20	.42
R 1	/R/	/**r**/	9,119	97.11
S 4	/S/	/**s**/	4,599	72.69
	/Z/	/**z**/	640	64.32
	/ZH/	/**ʒ**/	34	33.33
	/SH/	/**ʃ**/	20	1.30
T 3	/T/	/**t**/	7,528	96.59
	/CH/	/**ȼ**/	175	31.03
	/SH/	/**ʃ**/	30	1.95

Grapheme	Phoneme: Hanna symbol	SSA symbol	Frequency	Percent
U	/U3/	/**u**/	1,212	85.95
10	/U/	/**ɨu**/	814	68.51
	/ə/	/**ə**/	297	4.93
	/U2/	/**ə**/*	203	25.79
	/O7/	/**u**/	200	54.34
	/O6/	/**ɯ**/	93	20.52
	/W/	/**w**/	47	7.50
	/E5/	/**ə**/′	31	1.42
	/I3/	/**i**/	3	.03
	/E3/	/**e**/	2	.05
V	/V/	/**v**/	1,485	99.54
1				
W	/W/	/**w**/	578	92.35
1				
X	/KS/	/**ks**/	245	90.41
6	/K/	/**k**/	80	1.75
	/S/	/**s**/	77	1.21
	/G/	/**g**/	42	3.17
	/Z/	/**z**/	42	4.22
	/SH/	/**ʃ**/	3	.23
Y	/I3/	/**i**/	1,801	23.04
6	/I/	/**ȧ**/	211	14.23
	/Y/	/**y**/	53	44.17
	/ə/	/**ə**/	23	.38
	/E5/	/**ə**/′	4	.18
	/U2/	/**ə**/*	2	1.98
Z	/Z/	/**z**/	229	23.01
3	/S/	/**s**/	6	.14
	/ZH/	/**ʒ**/	2	1.98

Single letter totals

26	97		93,764	

Simple digraphs

Grapheme	Phoneme Hanna symbol	Phoneme SSA symbol	Frequency	Percent
AE	/E/	/**ɛ**/	5	.19
2	/E3/	/**e**/	1	.02
AH	/A5/	/**ɑ**/	4	.68
1				
AI	/A/	/**ɑ**/	208	9.25
6	/A2/	/**ɑ**/″	46	20.90
	/I3/	/**i**/	15	.19
	/ə/	/**ə**/	9	.14
	/E3/	/**e**/	4	.10
	/A3/	/**a**/	1	.02
AL	/L1/	/**l**/′	4	.61
1				
AO	/O2/	/**ɔ**/	2	.26
1				
AU	/O2/	/**ɔ**/	146	19.03
4	/A5/	/**ɑ**/	4	.68
	/O/	/**o**/	3	.11
	/ə/	/**ə**/	1	.01
AW	/O2/	/**ɔ**/	75	9.77
1				
AY	/A/	/**ɑ**/	131	5.82
4	/I/	/**ȧ**/	3	.20
	/E3/	/**e**/	1	.02
	/I3/	/**i**/	1	.01
BB	/B/	/**b**/	63	2.73
1				
BT	/T/	/**t**/	11	.14
1				
CC	/K/	/**k**/	76	1.61
1				
CE	/SH/	/**ʃ**/	2	.13
1				

Grapheme	Phoneme Hanna symbol	Phoneme SSA symbol	Frequency	Percent
CH	/CH/	**/ƈ/**	313	55.49
3	/K/	**/k/**	142	3.01
	/SH/	**/ʃ/**	34	2.21
CI	/SH/	**/ʃ/**	81	5.27
1				
CK	/K/	**/k/**	290	6.15
1				
CQ	/K/	**/k/**	3	.06
1				
CS	/KS/	**/ks/**	26	9.59
1				
CT	/T/	**/t/**	2	.02
1				
CZ	/Z/	**/z/**	1	.10
1				
DD	/D/	**/d/**	74	2.00
1				
DG	/J/	**/j/**	51	5.19
1				
DI	/J/	**/j/**	2	.20
1				
DJ	/J/	**/j/**	16	1.62
1				
EA	/E/	**/ɛ/**	245	9.65
9	/E3/	**/e/**	139	3.81
	/E2/	**/ɛ/′**	49	24.74
	/U2/	**/ə/***	29	3.68
	/A5/	**/ɑ/**	18	3.10
	/A/	**/a/**	14	.62
	/A2/	**/a/″**	13	5.90
	/ə/	**/ə/**	3	.04
	/I3/	**/i/**	1	.01

Grapheme	Phoneme: Hanna symbol	Phoneme: SSA symbol	Frequency	Percent
ED	/T/	/**t**/	28	.35
1				
EE	/E/	/**ɛ**/	249	9.81
3	/E2/	/**ɛ**/′	36	18.18
	/I3/	/**i**/	6	.07
EI	/E/	/**ɛ**/	16	.63
8	/A/	/**ɑ**/	14	.62
	/I3/	/**i**/	11	.14
	/I/	/**ȧ**/	6	.40
	/A2/	/**ɑ**/″	5	2.27
	/E2/	/**ɛ**/′	2	1.01
	/ə/	/**ə**/	2	.03
	/E3/	/**e**/	1	.02
EL	/L1/	/**l**/′	19	2.91
1				
EN	/N1/	/**n**/′	84	65.62
1				
EO	/ə/	/**ə**/	10	.16
3	/E3/	/**e**/	3	.08
	/E/	/**ɛ**/	2	.07
ES	/Z/	/**z**/	44	4.42
1				
ET	/A/	/**ɑ**/	9	.40
1				
EU	/U/	/**iɯ**/	28	2.35
4	/U2/	/**ə**/*	6	.76
	/O6/	/**ɯ**/	4	.88
	/O7/	/**u**/	1	.27
EW	/U/	/**iɯ**/	38	3.19
3	/O6/	/**ɯ**/	22	4.85
	/O/	/**o**/	3	.11
EY	/I3/	/**i**/	40	.51
5	/A/	/**ɑ**/	14	.62
	/E/	/**ɛ**/	6	.23

Grapheme	Phoneme: Hanna symbol	Phoneme: SSA symbol	Frequency	Percent
—EY	/A2/	**/ɑ/″**	1	.45
	/I/	**/ȧ/**	1	.06
FF	/F/	**/f/**	177	8.76
1				
FT	/F/	**/f/**	3	.14
1				
GG	/G/	**/g/**	67	5.00
2	/J/	**/j/**	2	.20
GH	/G/	**/g/**	10	.74
2	/F/	**/f/**	8	.39
GI	/J/	**/j/**	14	1.42
1				
GM	/M/	**/m/**	8	.22
1				
GN	/N/	**/n/**	32	.41
1				
GU	/G/	**/g/**	19	1.42
1				
IA	/ə/	**/ə/**	2	.03
1				
IE	/E/	**/ɛ/**	33	1.30
6	/I3/	**/i/**	29	.37
	/I/	**/ȧ/**	26	1.75
	/ə/	**/ə/**	22	.36
	/E2/	**/ɛ/′**	14	7.07
	/E3/	**/e/**	4	.10
IL	/L1/	**/l/′**	7	1.07
1				
IN	/N1/	**/n/′**	3	2.34
1				
KH	/K/	**/k/**	3	.06
1				

Grapheme	Phoneme		Frequency	Percent
	Hanna symbol	SSA symbol		
KN	/N/	/**n**/	41	.53
1				
LD	/D/	/**d**/	6	.17
1				
LE	/L1/	/**l**/′	620	95.23
1				
LF	/F/	/**f**/	9	.44
1				
LK	/K/	/**k**/	14	.29
1				
LL	/L/	/**l**/	489	9.07
1				
LM	/M/	/**m**/	17	.48
1				
LN	/L/	/**l**/	1	.01
1				
LV	/V/	/**v**/	4	.26
1				
MB	/M/	/**m**/	27	.77
1				
MM	/M/	/**m**/	140	3.99
1				
MN	/M/	/**m**/	7	.23
2	/N/	/**n**/	1	.01
NG	/NG/	/**ŋ**/	362	58.86
1				
NN	/N/	/**n**/	127	1.65
1				
OA	/O/	/**o**/	126	4.87
2	/O2/	/**ɔ**/	9	1.17

Grapheme	Phoneme: Hanna symbol	Phoneme: SSA symbol	Frequency	Percent
OE	/O/	**/o/**	13	.50
3	/E/	**/ɛ/**	5	.19
	/O6/	**/ɯ/**	4	.88
OH	/O/	**/o/**	4	.15
1				
OI	/OI/	**/ɔi/**	92	61.74
1				
OL	/L1/	**/l/′**	1	.18
1				
ON	/N1/	**/n/′**	41	32.04
1				
OO	/O6/	**/ɯ/**	173	38.18
4	/O7/	**/u/**	114	30.97
	/O/	**/o/**	9	.34
	/U3/	**/ʊ/**	7	.49
OU	/ə/	**/ə/**	336	5.58
9	/OU/	**/ɑu/**	227	55.91
	/U3/	**/ʊ/**	30	2.12
	/O/	**/o/**	29	1.12
	/O6/	**/ɯ/**	29	6.40
	/O7/	**/u/**	25	6.79
	/U2/	**/ə/***	21	2.66
	/W/	**/w/**	1	.15
	/E5/	**/ə/′**	1	.04
OW	/O/	**/o/**	124	4.79
3	/OU/	**/ɑu/**	119	29.31
	/O3/	**/ɒ/**	4	.24
OY	/OI/	**/ɔi/**	48	32.21
2	/I/	**/ȧ/**	1	.06
PB	/B/	**/b/**	1	.05
1				
PH	/F/	**/f/**	242	12.02
1				

Grapheme	Phoneme Hanna symbol	SSA symbol	Frequency	Percent
PN	/N/	/**n**/	3	.07
1				
PP	/P/	/**p**/	153	4.44
1				
PS	/S/	/**s**/	19	.30
1				
PT	/T/	/**t**/	2	.02
1				
QU	/KW/	/**kw**/	191	97.45
2	/K/	/**k**/	27	.57
RH	/R/	/**r**/	16	.17
1				
RR	/R/	/**r**/	207	2.20
1				
SC	/S/	/**s**/	77	1.21
4	/SH/	/**ʃ**/	6	.39
	/K/	/**k**/	3	.06
	/Z/	/**z**/	3	.30
SH	/SH/	/**ʃ**/	398	25.89
1				
SI	/ZH/	/**ʒ**/	50	49.01
2	/SH/	/**ʃ**/	38	2.47
SL	/L/	/**l**/	5	.11
1				
SS	/S/	/**s**/	442	6.98
3	/Z/	/**z**/	13	1.30
	/SH/	/**ʃ**/	9	.58
ST	/S/	/**s**/	33	.52
1				
SW	/S/	/**s**/	4	.06
1				

Grapheme	Phoneme Hanna symbol	Phoneme SSA symbol	Frequency	Percent
TG	/G/	/**g**/	1	.07
1				
TH	/T1/	/**ŧh**/	411	100.00
3	/T2/	/**ħ**/	149	100.00
	/T/	/**t**/	1	.01
TI	/SH/	/**ʃ**/	820	53.35
3	/CH/	/**ȼ**/	13	2.33
	/ZH/	/**ʒ**/	1	.98
TT	/T/	/**t**/	216	2.77
1				
TW	/T/	/**t**/	3	.08
1				
UE	/U/	/**ɯ̇**/	27	2.27
2	/O6/	/**ɯ**/	16	3.53
UI	/I3/	/**i**/	16	.20
3	/U/	/**ɯ̇**/	8	.67
	/O6/	/**ɯ**/	6	1.32
UO	/O6/	/**ɯ**/	2	.44
1				
UY	/I/	/**ȧ**/	3	.20
1				
WH	/HW/	/**hw**/	89	100.00
2	/H/	/**h**/	16	2.06
WR	/R/	/**r**/	48	.52
1				
ZZ	/Z/	/**z**/	23	2.33
1				

Simple digraph totals

Grapheme	Phoneme Hanna symbol	Phoneme SSA symbol	Frequency	Percent
100	182		10,825	

All other spellings

Grapheme	Phoneme Hanna symbol	Phoneme SSA symbol	Frequency	Percent
A-E	/A/	/**ɑ**/	790	35.14
8	/I3/	/**i**/	187	2.39
	/A3/	/**a**/	147	3.38
	/A2/	/**ɑ**/″	50	22.72
	/A5/	/**ɑ**/	31	5.34
	/O2/	/**ɔ**/	3	.39
	/ə/	/**ə**/	3	.04
	/E3/	/**e**/	1	.02
AI-E	/A/	/**ɑ**/	18	.80
3	/A2/	/**ɑ**/″	3	1.36
	/I/	/**ȧ**/	1	.06
AIGH	/A/	/**ɑ**/	4	.17
1				
AU-E	/O2/	/**ɔ**/	9	1.17
3	/O/	/**o**/	2	.07
	/A/	/**ɑ**/	1	.04
AUGH	/O2/	/**ɔ**/	12	1.56
1				
AWE†	/O2/	/**ɔ**/	2	.26
1				
AY-E	/A/	/**ɑ**/	1	.04
1				
CCH	/K/	/**k**/	1	.02
1				
CHT	/T/	/**t**/	2	.02
1				
CQU	/KW/	/**kw**/	5	2.55
1				

†AWE, EWE, EYE, and OWE (for /O/) are erroneously listed as AW–E, EW–E, EY–E, and OW–E respectively.

Grapheme	Phoneme Hanna symbol	SSA symbol	Frequency	Percent
E–E	/ə/	**/ə/**	101	1.67
9	/E3/	**/e/**	79	2.16
	/E/	**/ɛ/**	62	2.44
	/U2/	**/ə/***	41	5.20
	/A2/	**/ɑ/″**	34	15.45
	/E2/	**/ɛ/′**	27	13.63
	/A/	**/ɑ/**	6	.26
	/I3/	**/i/**	1	.01
	/E5/	**/ə/′**	1	.04
EA–E	/E/	**/ɛ/**	30	1.18
4	/U2/	**/ə/***	2	.25
	/E3/	**/e/**	1	.02
	/I3/	**/i/**	1	.01
EAU	/O/	**/o/**	6	.23
2	/U/	**/ɯ̇/**	5	.42
EE–E	/E/	**/ɛ/**	9	.35
1				
EI–E	/E/	**/ɛ/**	6	.23
2	/A/	**/ɑ/**	2	.08
EIGH	/A/	**/ɑ/**	18	.80
2	/I/	**/ɑ̇/**	3	.20
EOU	/ə/	**/ə/**	8	13
1				
EU–E	/U/	**/ɯ̇/**	1	.08
1				
EWE†	/U/	**/ɯ̇/**	1	.08
1				
EYE†	/I/	**/ɑ̇/**	7	.47
1				
GUE	/G/	**/g/**	21	1.56
1				

†AWE, EWE, EYE, and OWE (for /O/) are erroneously listed as AW–E, EW–E, EY–E, and OW–E respectively.

Grapheme	Phoneme: Hanna symbol	Phoneme: SSA symbol	Frequency	Percent
I-E	/I/	/ȧ/	555	37.44
5	/I3/	/i/	339	4.33
	/E/	/ɛ/	44	1.73
	/ə/	/ə/	6	.09
	/U2/	/ə/*	1	.12
IA-E	/I3/	/i/	3	.03
1				
IE-E	/E/	/ɛ/	23	.90
4	/ə/	/ə/	4	.06
	/E2/	/ɛ/′	3	1.51
	/I3/	/i/	1	.01
IEU	/U/	/ɯ̇/	4	.33
1				
IEW	/U/	/ɯ̇/	6	.50
1				
IGH	/I/	/ȧ/	88	5.93
1				
NGUE	/NG/	/ŋ/	2	.33
1				
O-E	/O/	/o/	370	14.30
8	/U3/	/ʊ/	26	1.84
	/ə/	/ə/	21	.34
	/O3/	/ɒ/	20	1.21
	/O2/	/ɔ/	17	2.21
	/O6/	/ɯ/	12	2.64
	/O5/	/ɒ/′	4	3.14
	/U2/	/ə/*	1	.12
OA-E	/O/	/o/	3	.11
1				
OI-E	/OI/	/ɔ̇/	8	5.36
2	/ə/	/ə/	2	.03
OO-E	/O6/	/ɯ/	12	2.64
1				

Grapheme	Phoneme Hanna symbol	Phoneme SSA symbol	Frequency	Percent
OU-E	/OU/	/ɑɪ/	54	13.30
4	/O/	/o/	10	.38
	/O6/	/ɯ/	3	.66
	/U2/	/ə/*	1	.12
OUGH	/O2/	/ɔ/	15	1.95
4	/O/	/o/	8	.30
	/OU/	/ɑɪ/	4	.98
	/O6/	/ɯ/	2	.44
OW-E	/OU/	/ɑɪ/	2	.49
1				
OWE†	/O/	/o/	1	.03
1				
OY-E	/OI/	/ɔɪ/	1	.67
1				
SCH	/S/	/s/	2	.03
2	/SH/	/ʃ/	2	.13
SCI	/SH/	/ʃ/	5	.32
1				
SSI	/SH/	/ʃ/	51	3.31
1				
TCH	/CH/	/c/	61	10.81
1				
U-E	/U/	/iɯ/	256	21.54
8	/O6/	/ɯ/	34	7.50
	/U3/	/ʊ/	23	1.63
	/E5/	/ə/′	23	1.05
	/O7/	/u/	11	2.98
	/U2/	/ə/*	10	1.27
	/ə/	/ə/	4	.06
	/I3/	/i/	3	.03
UI-E	/O6/	/ɯ/	4	.88
1				

†AWE, EWE, EYE, and OWE (for /O/) are erroneously listed as AW–E, EW–E, EY–E, and OW–E respectively.

Grapheme	Phoneme Hanna symbol	Phoneme SSA symbol	Frequency	Percent
Y-E	/I/	/**ȧ**/	23	1.55
2	/I3/	/**i**/	1	.01

All other spelling totals

44	99	3,935

Summary

Grapheme	Phoneme	Frequency
Single letters		
26	97	93,764
Simple digraphs		
100	182	10,825
All other spellings		
44	99	3,935
TOTALS		
170	378	108,524

Appendix B Supplementary data, not on single phonemes, for comparison with Hanna, Table 8

All single phonemes involved are included in totals of Appendix A

Hanna symbol	Grapheme	Symbol totals Oc	Symbol totals It	Grapheme totals Oc	Grapheme totals It	Initial Oc	Initial It	Medial Oc	Medial It	Final Oc	Final It	Syllabic Oc	Syllabic It
/HW/		1,359	48										
1	WH			1,359	48	1,359	48						
/H9/		105	17										
5	HA			1	1	1	1						
	HAU			3	1	3	1						
	HI			12	5	3	3					9	2
	HO			34	6	34	6						
	HOU			55	4	55	4						
/KS/		578	203										
5	CS			15	7					15	7		
	CKS			10	9					10	9		
	KS			43	22					43	22		
	LKS			3	1					3	1		
	X			507	164			68	8	439	156		

/**KW**/		372	105										
2	CQU			11	7	11	7						
	QU			361	98	333	87	28	11				
/**L1**/		1,132	312										
6	AL			1	1					1	1		
	IL			20	5	5	2	2	1	8	1	5	1
	L			2	2							2	2
	LE			1,106	301	52	29	112	51	684	180	258	41
	LL			2	2							2	2
	UAL			1	1	1	1						
/**M1**/		43	23										
1	M			43	23	3	3					40	20
/**N1**/		761	175										
4	EN			570	116	62	27	27	7	184	19	297	63
	IN			1	1							1	1
	N			84	29	66	19			4	2	15	8
	ON			105	29	7	5	19	4	47	13	32	7

Appendix C Phoneme-grapheme correspondences (Spellings of sounds)

On the 48-phoneme basis of the Revised Scientific Alphabet, as in Table 15 of *RF/Sounds*
Phonemes are arranged in the phonemic order used in Table 15 of *RF/Sounds*
Graphemes are arranged in alphabetic order

This table is to be read:
In the material examined, the phoneme /p/ is represented by 2 different graphemes. The phoneme occurs 7,638 times in 1,967 different items (syllables or words). Of these, the grapheme *p* represents 7,276 occurrences in 1,850 different items; of which 5,211 occurrences in 1,290 different items are as the first phoneme of the syllable, 813 occurrences in 265 different items are medial (neither the first nor last phoneme of the syllable), and 1,252 occurrences in 295 different items are as the last phoneme of the syllable.

Pho-neme	Graph-eme	Phoneme totals		Grapheme totals		Initial		Medial		Final		Syllabic	
		Oc	It	Oc	It	Oc	It	Oc	It	Oc	It	Oc	It
/p/		7,638	1,967										
2	p			7,276	1,850	5,211	1,290	813	265	1,252	295		
	pp			362	117	188	63	21	8	153	46		
/b/		6,721	1,152										
2	b			6,686	1,130	6,050	925	44	21	592	184		
	bb			35	22			4	3	31	19		
/t/		26,609	4,496										
9	bt			40	11			3	2	37	9		
	ch́t			1	1					1	1		
	ct			2	2					2	2		
	d			220	65					220	65		
	ed			442	140					442	140		
	pt			9	2			1	1	8	1		

—/**t**/	t			24,998	4,122	9,529	1,695	2,404	654	13,065	1,773
	tt			751	152	122	28	2	1	627	123
	tw			146	1	146	1				
/**d**/		15,723	3,052								
4	d			14,285	2,723	4,265	1,072	516	144	9,504	1,507
	dd			138	41	45	7	6	2	87	32
	ed			767	282					767	282
	ld			533	6					533	6
/**k**/		10,010	2,680								
11	c			6,403	1,775	4,323	1,126	722	210	1,358	439
	cc			144	45	113	35			41	10
	ch			122	47	60	27	49	12	13	8
	ck			452	151			88	43	364	108
	cq			15	10	11	7			4	3
	k			1,854	343	272	72	300	82	1,282	189
	lk			52	12			19	6	33	6
	q			377	110	333	87	28	11	16	12
	x			68	17					68	17
	½x			510	165			507	164	3	1
	½xi			13	5	1	1			12	4
/**g**/		2,794	636								
4	g			2,616	560	2,248	437	24	12	344	111
	gg			70	42	6	3	16	8	48	31
	gh			4	3	4	3				
	½x			104	31			103	30	1	1

Phoneme	Grapheme	Phoneme totals Oc	Phoneme totals It	Grapheme totals Oc	Grapheme totals It	Initial Oc	Initial It	Medial Oc	Medial It	Final Oc	Final It	Syllabic Oc	Syllabic It
/f/		6,889	1,131										
7	f			6,117	954	5,104	818	115	37	898	99		
	ff			510	102	178	39	9	8	323	55		
	ft			31	4					31	4		
	gh			59	8					59	8		
	lf			63	2					63	2		
	ph			108	60	80	42	6	5	22	13		
	pph			1	1					1	1		
/v/		8,417	905										
4	f			4,001	3					4,001	3		
	lv			1	1			1	1				
	v			4,403	899	1,630	447	341	86	2,432	366		
	ve			12	2					12	2		
/th/		1,396	213										
2	h			4	1					4	1		
	th			1,392	212	872	102	44	10	476	100		
/th/		12,757	114										
1	th			12,757	114	11,416	49	14	7	1,327	58		

/s/		17,081	4,162										
9	c			2,477	622	980	279	130	34	1,367	309		
	ps			2	2	2	2						
	s			12,822	2,974	6,663	1,485	1,846	352	4,313	1,137		
	sc			55	33	35	19			20	14		
	ss			1,156	342	118	45	79	26	959	271		
	st			35	17			1	1	34	16		
	sw			34	6	34	6						
	½x			495	162			71	10	424	152		
	z			5	4	1	1			4	3		
/z/		11,089	2,063										
7	s			10,695	1,902	432	119	181	40	10,074	1,740	8	3
	sc			8	5	7	4			1	1		
	ss			25	11	24	10			1	1		
	x			1	1	1	1						
	½x			103	30					103	30		
	z			247	107	81	26	68	29	98	52		
	zz			10	7					10	7		
/sh/		3,045	850										
15	c			17	11	17	11						
	ce			7	1	7	1						
	ch			38	11	36	9			2	2		
	ci			182	47	39	13			143	34		
	s			58	10	58	10						
	sc			2	1	2	1						

Pho-neme	Graph-eme	Phoneme totals Oc	Phoneme totals It	Grapheme totals Oc	Grapheme totals It	Initial Oc	Initial It	Medial Oc	Medial It	Final Oc	Final It	Syllabic Oc	Syllabic It
—/sh/	sci			17	5	15	4			2	1		
	sh			1,178	278	853	151	78	24	245	102	2	1
	si			22	15	22	15						
	ss			65	14	15	7			50	7		
	ssi			77	28					77	28		
	t			7	6	4	3			3	3		
	ti			1,360	418	1,157	379			203	39		
	½x			3	1	3	1						
	½xi			12	4	12	4						
/ʒ/		170	52										
5	g			6	5			2	1	4	4		
	s			78	20	30	7			48	13		
	si			81	24	34	14			47	10		
	½x			1	1	1	1						
	z			4	2	4	2						
/ch/		1,931	348										
5	ch			1,457	215	447	124	50	16	960	75		
	t			329	85	258	72			71	13		
	tch			85	36			12	4	73	32		
	te			4	2	4	2						
	ti			56	10	56	10						

/j/		1,582	492										
10	d			38	16	4	3			34	13		
	de			2	2	2	2						
	dg			95	35			9	7	86	28		
	di			42	6	42	6						
	dj			7	6	7	6						
	g			948	306	299	113	70	18	579	175		
	ge			4	2	4	2						
	gg			2	1					2	1		
	gi			30	7	19	4			11	3		
	j			414	111	411	109			3	2		
/**m**/		10,281	1,820										
5	lm			17	5					17	5		
	m			10,049	1,727	5,698	926	554	155	3,757	626	40	20
	mb			13	9			5	3	8	6		
	mm			182	70	110	34	1	1	71	35		
	mn			20	9			10	4	10	5		
/**n**/		26,982	4,410										
9	en			570	116	62	27	27	7	184	19	297	63
	gn			66	19			21	8	45	11		
	in			1	1							1	1
	kn			259	21	259	21						
	n			25,727	4,168	3,539	625	8,453	1,212	13,720	2,325	15	8
	nd			2	2					2	2		
	nn			249	54	61	19	5	2	183	33		

Phoneme	Grapheme	Phoneme totals Oc	Phoneme totals It	Grapheme totals Oc	Grapheme totals It	Initial Oc	Initial It	Medial Oc	Medial It	Final Oc	Final It	Syllabic Oc	Syllabic It
—/n/	on			105	29	7	5	19	4	47	13	32	7
	pn			3	1	3	1						
/ŋ/		3,550	1,035										
3	n			385	123			294	70	91	53		
	nd			1	1					1	1		
	ng			3,164	911			202	56	2,962	855		
/l/		13,940	3,274										
7	al			1	1					1	1		
	il			20	5	5	2	2	1	8	1	5	1
	l			10,288	2,621	4,214	990	3,110	882	2,962	747	2	2
	le			1,106	301	52	29	112	51	684	180	258	41
	ll			2,519	342	148	56	174	50	2,195	234	2	2
	sl			5	3	3	2			2	1		
	ual			1	1	1	1						
/r/		25,471	5,424										
10	l			5	3					5	3		
	r			24,911	5,237	3,412	1,015	9,271	2,406	12,228	1,816		
	re			8	1					8	1		
	½re			13	10			6	4	7	6		
	rh			5	5	5	5						
	rps			5	1					5	1		
	rr			400	143	99	36	31	11	270	96		

—/**r**/	rrh			1	1	1	1				
	rt			1	1					1	1
	wr			122	22	122	22				
/**w**/		7,741	553								
5	½o-e			450	5	450	5				
	½oi			1	1			1	1		
	u			404	119	11	9	393	110		
	w			5,527	380	5,335	330	192	50		
	½wh			1,359	48			1,359	48		
/**y**/		2,260	250								
6	½ew			1	1	1	1				
	i			145	36	144	35	1	1		
	½u			357	148	357	148				
	½u-e			182	18	182	18				
	½ue			68	7	68	7				
	y			1,507	40	1,507	40				
/**h**/		6,759	484								
3	h			5,023	427	5,023	427				
	wh			377	9	377	9				
	½wh			1,359	48	1,359	48				

Consonant phoneme subtotals

24	145	230,836	41,564

Pho-neme	Graph-eme	Phoneme totals Oc	Phoneme totals It	Grapheme totals Oc	Grapheme totals It	Initial Oc	Initial It	Medial Oc	Medial It	Final Oc	Final It	Syllabic Oc	Syllabic It
/a/		13,059	1,443										
3	a			12,409	1,426	5,862	274	5,852	936	16	6	679	210
	a-e			643	14	3	2	640	12				
	ua			7	3			7	3				
/æ/		1,196	140										
9	a			32	13			32	13				
	a-e			196	54			196	54				
	ai			127	30	27	5	100	25				
	ai-e			7	4	5	2	2	2				
	aye			1	1			1	1				
	e			4	1			4	1				
	e-e			464	24	1	1	463	23				
	ea			46	11			46	11				
	ei			319	2			319	2				
/ɑ/		793	122										
3	a			765	110	220	15	545	95				
	a-e			22	9			22	9				
	au			6	3	1	1	5	2				
/ɑ/		77	28										
2	a			76	27	22	5	38	10	16	12		
	e			1	1	1	1						

/ā/		1,754	304										
9	a			1,013	253	156	42	813	199	43	11	1	1
	a-e			661	22	549	2	112	20				
	aa			3	1			3	1				
	ah			10	1							10	1
	au			17	6			17	6				
	e			3	1			3	1				
	ea			31	11			31	11				
	½oi			1	1					1	1		
	ua			15	8			15	8				
/e/		12,709	3,172										
10	a			371	10	261	7	104	1	6	2		
	ai			298	4			298	4				
	ay			52	1			52	1				
	e			10,987	2,941	3,315	1,159	7,538	1,749	41	15	93	18
	e-e			530	96	314	36	216	60				
	e-ue			7	4	3	1	4	3				
	ea			402	105			402	105				
	ie			40	5			40	5				
	u			1	1			1	1				
	ue			21	5			21	5				
/ē/		6,574	1,306										
17	a			2,117	637	75	41	468	170	1,123	355	451	71
	a-e			1,722	301	46	19	1,674	280	2	2		

Pho-neme	Graph-eme	Phoneme totals Oc	Phoneme totals It	Grapheme totals Oc	Grapheme totals It	Initial Oc	Initial It	Medial Oc	Medial It	Final Oc	Final It	Syllabic Oc	Syllabic It
—/e/	a-ue			2	1			2	1				
	ai			779	214	55	12	715	196				
	ai-e			22	7	1	1	21	6				
	aigh			22	5			22	5				
	au-e			1	1			1	1				
	ay			1,109	90			197	25	912	65		
	e			3	2			2	1	1	1		
	e			1	1					1	1		
	ea			198	9			198	9				
	ee			1	1					1	1		
	eh			1	1							1	1
	ei			4	4			4	4				
	eigh			82	19	10	4	47	7	25	8		
	ey			508	12			20	5	488	7		
	ue			2	1			2	1				
/ɪ/		16,340	4,217										
18	a			29	15	16	9	13	6				
	a-e			296	94	169	53	127	41				
	ai			77	15			75	13	1	1	1	1
	e			4,994	798	62	7	5	2	4,555	645	372	144

—/ɪ/	e-e			10	4	3	1	7	3				
	ee			37	4			1	1	1	1	35	2
	ei			22	3	21	2	1	1				
	ey			102	22	3	2	5	5	30	10	64	5
	hi			9	2							9	2
	i			6,060	2,185	2,953	1,014	757	288	933	444	1,417	439
	i-e			315	100	55	20	260	80				
	ia			7	3	6	2			1	1		
	ia-e			7	2	7	2						
	ie			338	121	83	19	252	100	3	2		
	oi			1	1							1	1
	u-e			30	3	30	3						
	ui			3	2	1	1	2	1				
	y			4,003	843			17	8	2,705	630	1,281	205
/i/		15,136	1,746										
9	e			32	6			32	6				
	ee			330	2			330	2				
	hi			3	3	3	3						
	i			14,216	1,622	6,593	468	7,591	1,134	6	6	26	14
	i-e			222	51	3	2	219	49				
	o			48	2			48	2				
	u			104	4			104	4				
	ui			84	14			84	14				
	y			97	42			97	42				

Pho-neme	Graph-eme	Phoneme totals Oc	Phoneme totals It	Grapheme totals Oc	Grapheme totals It	Initial Oc	Initial It	Medial Oc	Medial It	Final Oc	Final It	Syllabic Oc	Syllabic It
/ɪ/		7,845	835										
20	ae			1	1					1	1		
	e			4,064	206	95	2	51	27	3,873	165	45	12
	e-e			444	46	27	5	417	41				
	e'e			1	1	1	1						
	ea			1,385	266	153	18	1,068	210	155	35	9	3
	ea-e			175	27	10	3	165	24				
	ea-ue			5	1			5	1				
	ee			1,158	175	12	5	860	141	284	27	2	2
	ee-e			10	6			10	6				
	ei			72	13			13	6	23	6	36	1
	ei-e			64	11			64	11				
	eo			180	3					180	3		
	ey			3	2			1	1	2	1		
	i			16	8			13	5	3	3		
	i-e			63	14	1	1	62	13				
	i-ue			4	3			4	3				
	ie			111	36			111	36				
	ie-e			87	14			87	14				
	oe			1	1					1	1		
	ui			1	1					1	1		
/ɵ/		10,521	1,103										
7	a			1,215	35			1,215	35				

—/ɵ/	au			42	9	3	2					39	7
	ho			34	6	34	6						
	o			9,150	1,022	5,190	116	3,652	817	189	59	119	30
	o-e			35	21			35	21				
	o-ue			13	5			13	5				
	ow			32	5			32	5				
/ŏ/		4,691	442										
13	a			1,424	107	706	18	663	81	55	8		
	a-e			9	4			9	4				
	ao			3	1			3	1				
	au			69	38	2	2	22	12	6	5	39	19
	au-e			161	7			161	7				
	augh			32	8			27	6	5	2		
	aw			184	34			45	11	115	21	24	2
	awe			1	1							1	1
	hau			3	1	3	1						
	o			2,595	219	693	35	1,902	184				
	o-e			43	10			43	10				
	oa			15	3			15	3				
	ough			152	9			152	9				
/ʊ/		6,273	1,118										
10	o			857	104	261	6	596	98				
	o-e			565	34			565	34				
	½o-e			450	5			450	5				
	o-ue			6	2			6	2				

Phoneme	Grapheme	Phoneme totals		Grapheme totals		Initial		Medial		Final		Syllabic	
		Oc	It	Oc	It	Oc	It	Oc	It	Oc	It	Oc	It
—/ʊ/	oe			63	2			63	2				
	oo			17	7			17	7				
	ou			527	157	135	70	391	86				
	u			3,768	797	1,076	227	2,591	545	101	25		
	u-e			19	9			19	9				
	u-ue			1	1			1	1				
/ʊ̲/		2,238	370										
12	e			647	94	2	2	645	92				
	e-e			360	27			360	27				
	ea			142	29	63	10	79	19				
	ea-e			1	1			1	1				
	eu			4	4			4	4				
	i			328	55			328	55				
	o			351	39			351	39				
	o-e			11	1			11	1				
	o-o			5	3			5	3				
	ou			16	6			16	6				
	u			356	101	6	3	350	98				
	u-e			17	10	5	2	12	8				
/ə/		17,172	2,904										
19	a			5,602	1,105	845	229	1,117	334	471	213	3,169	329
	a-e			148	51	47	22	101	29				

—/ə/	e			8,766	958	2,463	565	1,873	379	4,410	10	20	4
	ea			1	1	1	1						
	eo			3	1	3	1						
	eu			2	2			2	2				
	ha			1	1	1	1						
	i			2	2	1	1					1	1
	½i-o			8	3	8	3						
	io			3	2	3	2						
	o			2,550	748	650	172	1,894	572	3	3	3	1
	o-e			49	4	1	1	48	3				
	oi			1	1	1	1						
	ou			6	5	1	1	5	4				
	½re			13	10			13	10				
	u			13	6	2	1	11	5				
	ue			2	2	1	1	1	1				
	uo			1	1	1	1						
	y			1	1			1	1				
/o/		1,198	414										
7	au			5	3			1	1	4	2		
	o			1,016	364	4	2	18	4	715	244	279	114
	oa			1	1					1	1		
	oe			19	6	1	1	18	5				
	ot			6	2			5	1	1	1		
	ough			7	3					2	1	5	2
	ow			144	35	39	11	8	1	11	3	86	20

Pho-neme	Graph-eme	Phoneme totals Oc	Phoneme totals It	Grapheme totals Oc	Grapheme totals It	Initial Oc	Initial It	Medial Oc	Medial It	Final Oc	Final It	Syllabic Oc	Syllabic It
/ō/		4,893	774										
18	au			2	1					2	1		
	au-e			1	1			1	1				
	eau			6	1					6	1		
	eo			1	1					1	1		
	ew			7	5			4	2	3	3		
	o			2,568	391	304	6	865	186	1,164	156	235	43
	o-e			1,199	183	3	2	1,193	180	3	1		
	o-ue			1	1			1	1				
	oa			242	71	13	6	229	65				
	oa-e			7	4			7	4				
	oe			19	7			14	4	5	3		
	oh			53	1							53	1
	oo			27	6			27	6				
	ou			117	21			117	21				
	ou-e			56	4			56	4				
	ough			58	4					58	4		
	ow			527	71	93	7	113	24	315	39	6	2
	owe			2	1							2	1
/u/		2,577	466										
11	½ew			1	1					1	1		
	o			368	14			1	1	367	13		
	oo			388	54			388	54				

—/u/	ou			546	8			546	8				
	u			604	171	7	4	377	101	111	39	109	27
	½u			257	117			12	5	245	112		
	u-e			297	78	56	12	241	66				
	½u-e			57	9			57	9				
	ue			40	9	19	4	2	2	2	1	17	2
	½ue			18	4			16	3	2	1		
	ugh			1	1							1	1
/û/		6,051	322										
19	eu			1	1					1	1		
	ew			22	12			4	4	18	8		
	o			3,645	26			59	13	3,586	13		
	o-e			112	15			112	15				
	oe			11	5			4	2	7	3		
	oeu			1	1					1	1		
	oo			430	88	1	1	370	84	59	3		
	oo-e			11	6	1	1	10	5				
	ou			1,127	36			339	26	788	10		
	ou-e			23	4			23	4				
	ough			92	2					92	2		
	u			161	48			77	19	84	29		
	½u			100	30			39	9	61	21		
	u-e			79	19			79	19				
	½u-e			125	9			97	8	28	1		
	ue			44	5			2	2	42	3		
	½ue			51	4			5	2	46	2		
	ui			15	10			15	10				
	ui-e			1	1			1	1				

Pho-neme	Graph-eme	Phoneme totals Oc	Phoneme totals It	Grapheme totals Oc	Grapheme totals It	Initial Oc	Initial It	Medial Oc	Medial It	Final Oc	Final It	Syllabic Oc	Syllabic It
/ɑi/		5,961	859										
14	ai-e			2	1	2	1						
	eigh			57	4	33	1	6	2			18	1
	eye			55	4	36	2					19	2
	i			2,107	302	71	11	529	149	274	120	1,233	22
	i-e			1,802	324	78	25	1,724	299				
	½i-o			8	3							8	3
	ie			153	49			139	43	14	6		
	igh			546	74			447	63	99	11		
	ui			1	1			1	1				
	ui-e			6	5			6	5				
	uy			37	6			2	2	35	4		
	y			1,154	73			3	3	1,151	70		
	y-e			31	11			31	11				
	ye			2	2			1	1	1	1		
/ɵɪ/		347	105										
3	oi			165	66	21	2	135	56	9	8		
	oi-e			30	7			30	7				
	oy			152	32			51	6	101	26		
/ɑu/		2,312	256										
5	hou			55	4	55	4						
	ou			1,422	150	690	34	678	111	54	5		
	ou-e			194	40	1	1	96	19	97	20		
	ough			9	6			7	4	2	2		
	ow			632	56			169	28	463	28		

/iu/		59	33						
5	eu			3	1			3	1
	ieu			2	2			2	2
	iew			8	3	7	2	1	1
	u			45	26			45	26
	ue			1	1			1	1
/iū/		1,079	289						
9	eau			24	3			24	3
	eu			15	2			15	2
	eu-e			1	1	1	1		
	ew			229	19	30	4	199	15
	iew			35	5	2	2	33	3
	u			453	160	138	39	315	121
	u-e			248	81	248	81		
	ue			52	13	8	4	44	9
	ui			22	5	22	5		
Vowel phoneme subtotals									
24	252	140,855	22,760						

Summary

Consonant phoneme subtotals			
24	145	230,836	41,564
Vowel phoneme subtotals			
24	252	140,855	22,768
TOTALS			
48	397	371,691	64,332

Appendix D Spellings in Appendix C not found in *How we spell!* (1969 revision)

Phoneme	Grapheme	As in
/ʼn/	en	sudd*en*[1]
/ʼn/	in	bas*in*[1]
/ʼn/	on	pard*on*[1]
/ʼl/	al	med*al*s[1]
/ʼl/	il	ev*il*[1]
/ʼl/	le	peop*le*[1]
/ʼl/	ual	vict*ual*s[1]
/y/	½ew	sin*ew*[2]
/y/	½u	partic*u*lar[2]
/y/	½u-e	distrib*ute*[2]
/y/	½ue	contin*ue*[2]
/ı/	oi	conn*oi*sseur[3]
/ɒ/	au	*au*xiliary[3]
/u/	½ew	sin*ew*[2]
/u/	½u	partic*u*lar[2]
/u/	½u-e	distrib*ute*[2]
/u/	ue	iss*ue*[3]
/u/	½ue	contin*ue*[2]
/ū/	½u	*u*nion[2]
/ū/	½u-e	*u*s*e*d[2]
/ū/	½ue	val*ue*[2]
/iu/	ieu	l*ieu*tenant[3]

Notes

[1] *RF/Sounds* treated these phonemes as syllabic consonants, whereas most current dictionaries insert a preceding schwa.

[2] *RF/Sounds* treated these phonemes as /yu/ or /yū/, whereas the *American College Dictionary* (the basis for *How we spell!*) treats them as /ɯ/, in agreement with the SSA phonemic alphabet.

[3] These 4 words involve slight divergencies between *RF/Sounds* and current practice.

Not included in Appendix C, nor in this table, are less than a dozen words occurring in *RF/Sounds*, either involving non-English sounds; e.g.

/ṅ/	as in	fia*n*ce
/ü/	"	n*u*ances
/yū/	"	mons*ieu*r

or spelled, in the material examined, with special characters not now commonly employed; e.g.

/æ/	as in	pæan	now commonly	paean
/aï/	"	naïve	" "	naive
/ö/	"	zoölogists	"	zoologists

Appendix E WES—spelling reform version

World English Spelling (WES)

A no-new-letter phonemic notation for English

The English language, cosmopolitan in vocabulary and relatively simple in grammar, is uniquely suitable for international use as a second language—a purpose to which it is being increasingly applied. English spelling is, however, almost unbelievably irregular and confusing. A recent compilation, *English heterography,* lists over 500 different spellings of the 41 sounds which it distinguishes—an average of over 12 spellings per sound —and the different pronunciations of the spellings are no less confusing. This irregularity has been the chief obstacle to even more rapid spread of English as the chief international auxiliary language.

World English Spelling offers substantially one spelling for each sound, one pronunciation for each spelling. It accomplishes this result with:

1) No new letters;

2) No diacritics (which, in effect, create new letters, for typing or printing);

3) As little disturbance of familiar forms and usages as practicable. Over 40 words out of 100 on the printed page retain precisely their present spellings.

World English Spelling is the outcome of long study and large experience by the Simplified Spelling Society in Great Britain since 1910, and by the Simpler Spelling Association in the United States since 1946. It has been developed as the soundest, most practicable basis for spelling reform for the English-speaking peoples, but that phase probably lies one or two generations in the future. Meantime, WES is immediately available for use as an auxiliary medium of international communication.

This folder gives all essential information for immediate practical use of World English Spelling.

World English Spelling
(WES)

Symbol	*As in*
a	at, man; ask; about, data
aa	alms, father, bah; (ask)
ae	age, main, say; air
ar	army, market, far
au	author, law, all, water, ought
b	bay, rubber, cab
ch	check, church, watch
d	down, ladder, bid
e	edge, men, said, head, any
ee	each, here, see, be
er	further, collar, motor, murmur
f	fast, office, photograph, safe
g	game, ragged, bag
h	had, behind, who
i	it, him, pretty, give; any
ie	ice, tie, kind, might, by
j	just, general, stage, judge
k	can, keep, account, back
l	late, fellow, deal
m	might, common, them
n	night, dinner, then
ng	thing, long, going, single
nk	think, bank, uncle, ankle

Symbol	*As in*
o	on, bother, not; was, what
oe	old, note, goes, so, coal, show
oi	oil, point, boy
oo	fool, move, group, rule, too
or	order, north, for; story, more
ou	out, pound, now, bough
p	pay, happy, cap
r	rate, married, dear
s	seal, lesson, city, race, base
sh	shall, pressure, nation, wish
t	town, letter, bit
th	that, rather, with
thh	thought, nothing, both
u	up, other, but, some, touch
ue	use, your, music, due, few
ur	further, her, early, first work
uu	full, sure, should, good
v	vast, never, save
w	wet, forward, one, quick
wh	which, everywhere
y	yet, beyond, million
z	zeal, puzzle, is, raise, size
zh	jabot, pleasure, vision, rouge

Separate by a dot successive letters which might otherwise be read as a digraph —

short.hand, mis.hap, en.gaej, man.kiend

gae.eti, ree.elect, hie.est, loe.er, influu.ens, pou.er, emploi.ee

Linkon'z Getizberg Adres

Forskor and seven yeerz agoe our faatherz braut forthh on this kontinent a nue naeshon, konseevd in liberti, and dedikaeted to the propozishon that aul men ar kreeaeted eekwal.

Nou wee ar en.gaejd in a graet sivil wor, testing whether that naeshon, or eni naeshon soe konseevd and soe dedikaeted, kan long enduer. Wee ar met on a graet batlfeeld ov that wor. Wee hav kum to dedikaet a porshon ov that feeld az a fienal resting-plaes for thoez hoo heer gaev thaer lievz that that naeshon miet liv. It iz aultogether fiting and proper that wee shuud doo this.

But in a larjer sens, wee kanot dedikaet—wee kanot konsekraet—wee kanot haloe—this ground. The braev men, living and ded, hoo strugld heer, hav konsekraeted it far abuv our poor pou.er to ad or detrakt. The wurld wil litl noet nor long remember whot wee sae heer, but it kan never forget whot thae did heer. It iz for us, the living, rather, to bee dedikaeted heer to the unfinisht wurk which thae hoo faut heer hav thus far soe noebli advanst. It iz rather for us to bee heer dedikaeted to the graet task remaening befor us—that from theez onord ded wee taek inkreest devoeshon to that kauz for which thae gaev the last fuul mezher ov devoeshon; that wee heer hieli rezolv that theez ded shal not hav died in vaen; that this naeshon, under God, shal hav a nue burthh ov freedom; and that guvernment ov the peepl, bie the peepl, for the peepl, shal not perish from the urthh.

Notes

The short vowel sounds are spelled **a e i o u uu**, as in *That pen iz not much guud.*

A stressed short **a** or **o** before **r** is distinguished by doubling the **r** — *karri, forren* (compare *kar, for*).

The name sounds of the vowel letters are spelled with a following *e* — **ae ee ie oe ue**, as in *Thae seem liek soe fue.*

The remaining long vowels and diphthongs are spelled **aa au oi oo ou**, as in *Faather taut boiz thhroo sound.*

Except as a part of **ch**, *c q x* are used only in proper names.

The unstressed neutral vowel heard in *a*bout furth*e*r dat*a* has no exact equivalent in World English Spelling, but is nearest to **u**. When this sound is stressed (which occurs only before **r**), write **u** — *wurk, further*. Initially or finally, retain the **a** of conventional spelling — *about, daeta*. Medially, retain any single vowel of the conventional spelling, especially where the vowel may be stressed with its normal value in derivatives — *organ, organik; rezident, rezidenshal; authhor, authhorriti;* etc. In the termination most commonly spelled -tion, write **o** — *naeshon*. Write *the, a,* and *to* (which are usually pronounced with the unstressed neutral vowel) as in traditional orthography.

Write the symbol for **r** wherever r-keepers (as Webster's Third New International calls them) would pronounce it.

Prefer, in general, as a guide to WES word forms the pronunciations heard in careful, deliberate speech.

In a slightly modified form, described in *World English Spelling (WES) for better reading* (free on request), WES enormously simplifies the task of learning to read and write the English language. This is true even when it is used only as a medium for the first teaching of reading and writing, to be followed by learning to read and write in the present traditional orthography.

Simpler Spelling Association
Lake Placid Club, N.Y. 12946

10SSA15S68 **Printed in the U.S.A.**